# 1 TIMOTHY

# DISCOVER TOGETHER BIBLE STUDY SERIES

*1 Peter: Discovering Encouragement in Troubling Times*

*1 Timothy: Discovering Clarity in a World That Can't Agree*

*1 and 2 Thessalonians: Discovering Hope in a Promised Future*

*Daniel: Discovering the Courage to Stand for Your Faith*

*Ecclesiastes: Discovering Meaning in a Meaningless World*

*Ephesians: Discovering Your Identity and Purpose in Christ*

*Galatians: Discovering Freedom in Christ Through Daily Practice*

*Hosea: Discovering God's Fierce Love*

*Isaiah: Discovering Assurance Through Prophecies About Your Mighty King*

*James: Discovering the Joy of Living Out Your Faith*

*Luke: Discovering Healing in Jesus's Words to Women*

*Philippians: Discovering Joy Through Relationship*

*Proverbs: Discovering Ancient Wisdom for a Postmodern World, Volume 1*

*Proverbs: Discovering Ancient Wisdom for a Postmodern World, Volume 2*

*Psalms: Discovering Authentic Worship*

*Revelation: Discovering Life for Today and Eternity*

*Ruth: Discovering God's Faithfulness in an Anxious World*

*Leader's guides are available at www.discovertogetherseries.com*

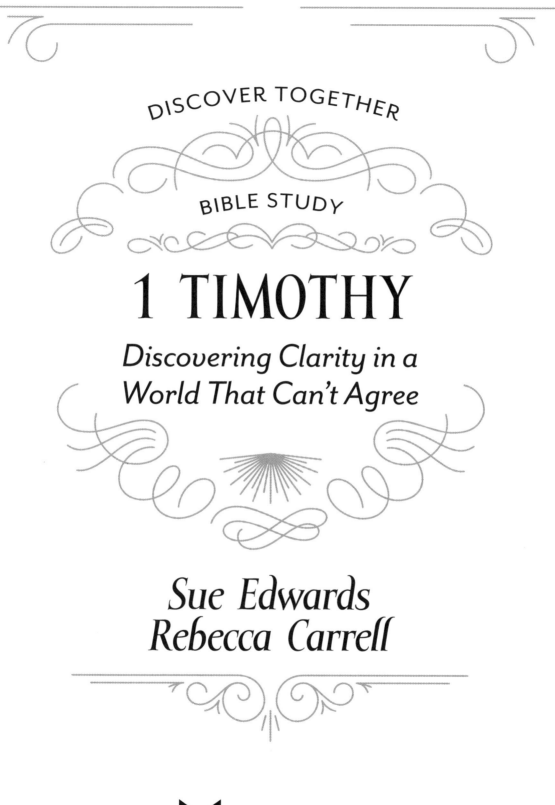

DISCOVER TOGETHER

BIBLE STUDY

# 1 TIMOTHY

*Discovering Clarity in a World That Can't Agree*

## Sue Edwards
## Rebecca Carrell

KREGEL
PUBLICATIONS

*1 Timothy: Discovering Clarity in a World That Can't Agree*
© 2023 by Sue Edwards and Rebecca Carrell

Published by Kregel Publications, a division of Kregel Inc., 2450 Oak Industrial Dr. NE, Grand Rapids, MI 49505. www.kregel.com.

With gratitude for contributions by interns Lisa Adams and Linda Teel.

Cataloging-in-Publication Data is available from the Library of Congress.

ISBN 978-0-8254-4827-0

Printed in the United States of America
23  24  25  26  27  28  29  30  31  32  /  5  4  3  2  1

# Contents

# Why Study the Bible?

Varied voices perpetually shout for our attention. Who should we listen to? Who can we believe? The Uber driver we've never met but count on to take us home? The man hawking cell phones behind the counter? The woman on the treadmill beside us? Maybe we can trust them; maybe we can't. Over time we can discern whether or not we're comfortable inviting them into our personal space or giving weight to their opinions. But the reality is that ultimately everyone will disappoint us, and we will disappoint them too.

Only One is perfectly trustworthy. Only One offers a way to combat the chaos rocking our world right now. Only One sent us a Love Letter that leads to peace and stability despite the chaos that surrounds us. "All Scripture is God-breathed and is useful for teaching, rebuking, correcting and training in righteousness, so that the servant of God may be thoroughly equipped for every good work" (2 Timothy 3:16–17).

Years ago a wise woman, who secretly paid for my (Sue's) daughters to attend a Christian school we couldn't afford, planted that truth in my mind and heart. This concept blossomed into realistic expectations and a hearty hunger for a relationship with that trustworthy One. That hunger led to a lifetime of savoring God's Love Letter, the Scriptures, and that relationship and practice upended everything. Wherever you are in your journey, Jesus invites you to experience the contentment and peace that only he can provide, regardless of your circumstances.

Jesus promised, "Peace I leave with you; my peace I give you. I do not give to you as the world gives. Do not let your hearts be troubled and do not be afraid" (John 14:27). Engage with us so that together we can combat whatever chaos is invading our lives right now.

# How to Get the Most Out of a Discover Together Bible Study

We're all at different junctures in our spiritual migrations, but God's Word doesn't separate us according to superficial differences. We all want to know God intimately and flourish, and we can all learn from one another. "As iron sharpens iron, so one person sharpens another" (Proverbs 27:17).

Discover Together Bible studies are designed to promote unity, for all women to learn from and enjoy together regardless of age, stage, race, nationality, spiritual maturity, economic or educational status. God proclaims we are all sisters in his forever family preparing to spend eternity together (Matthew 12:46–50).

However, our schedules vary week to week depending on needs of loved ones, travel responsibilities, and work demands. To honor these differences, this study provides two choices:

1. Basic questions that require between one and one and a half hours of prep a week, offering in-depth Bible study with a minimum time commitment;
2. "Digging Deeper" questions for women who want to probe the text more deeply.

Women wanting to tackle the "Digging Deeper" questions may

- need resources such as an atlas, Bible dictionary, or concordance;
- check online resources and compare parallel passages for additional insight;
- use an interlinear Greek-English text or *Vine's Expository Dictionary* to do word studies;
- grapple with complex theological issues and differing views; and
- create outlines and charts and write essays worthy of seminarians.

In addition to God's Love Letter, we also need authentic community, a place to be ourselves, where we are loved unconditionally despite our differences and challenged to grow.

This Bible study is designed for both individual and group discovery, but you will benefit more if you tackle each week's lesson on your own and then meet with other women to share insights, struggles, and aha moments.

If you choose to meet together, someone needs to lead the group. You will find a free, downloadable leader's guide for each study, along with tips for facilitating small groups with excellence, at discovertogetherseries .com.

Choose a realistic level of Bible study that fits your schedule. You may want to finish the basic questions first and then dig deeper as time permits. Take time to savor the questions, and don't rush through the application.

Read the sidebars for additional insight to enrich your experience. Note the optional passage to memorize and determine if this discipline would be helpful for you.

Do not allow yourself to be intimidated by women who have walked with the Lord longer, who have more time, or who are gifted differently. You bring something to the table no one else can contribute.

Prioritize your study. Consider spacing your study throughout the week to allow time to ponder and meditate on what the Holy Spirit is teaching you. Do not make other appointments during the group Bible study. Ask God to enable you to attend faithfully.

Come with an excitement to learn from others and a desire to share yourself and your journey. Give it your best to find the only One who will never let you down.

## WHAT IS INDUCTIVE STUDY, AND WHY IS IT SO POWERFUL?

The Discover Together series uses inductive Bible study as a structure to dig into the Bible. Inductive study is the practice of investigating or interviewing a Bible passage to determine its true meaning, attempting to leave behind any presuppositions or personal agendas.

First, we seek to learn what the original author meant when writing to the original audience. We carefully examine the words and ideas. We ask questions like, What is happening? Who is it happening to? And where is it happening? Only after we answer those questions are we ready to discern what we think God meant.

Once we are clear about what God meant, then we are ready to apply these truths to our present circumstances, trusting that a steady diet of truth will result in an enriched relationship with Almighty God and beneficial changes in our character, actions, and attitudes.

Inductive study is powerful because discerning biblical truth is the best way we grow in faith, thrive in our lives, and deepen our relationship with the God who created us.

To experience this powerful process, we must immerse ourselves in this practice as a lifestyle—and not just focus on a verse here and there. Our life goal must be to digest the Bible, whole book by whole book, as life-giving nourishment that cannot be attained any other way.

Over a span of sixteen hundred years, God orchestrated the creation of sixty-six biblical documents written by the Holy Spirit through more than forty human authors who came from different backgrounds. Together they produced a unified Love Letter that communicates without error God's affection, grace, direction, truth, and wisdom. He did this so that we would not be left without access to his mind and heart.[1]

## THE INCREDIBLE BENEFITS OF BIBLICAL LITERACY

Earning a quality education changes us. It makes us literate and alters our futures. Many of us sacrifice years, money, and energy to educate ourselves because we understand education's benefits and rewards.

Biblical literacy is even more valuable than secular education! But just like with secular learning, becoming biblically literate requires serious investment. However, the life-changing rewards and benefits far outweigh a diploma and increased lifetime earnings from the most prestigious Ivy League university.

A few benefits include

- a more intimate relationship with Almighty God;
- an understanding of the way the world works and how to live well in it;
- a supernatural ability to love ourselves and others;
- insight into our own sin nature along with a path to overcome it, and when we fail, a way to wipe the shame slate clean, pick ourselves up forgiven, and move on with renewed hope;
- relational health experienced in community;
- support through struggles;
- continued growth in becoming a person who exhibits the fruit of the Spirit: love, joy, peace, patience, kindness, goodness, faithfulness, gentleness, and self-control (Galatians 5:22–23); and
- contentment as we learn to trust in God's providential care.

Every book of the Bible provides another layer in the scaffolding of truth that transforms our mind, heart, attitudes, and actions. What truths wait to be unearthed in this letter to Timothy, and how will they change us?

# Why Study 1 Timothy?

In 2002, fashion designer Marc Jacobs invited Japanese artist Takashi Murakami to collaborate on a remodel of Louis Vuitton's luxury handbags. Traditionally identified by their brown leather and beige brand stamp, the new purses were white and boasted the iconic monogram in vibrant pinks, yellows, blues, and greens and debuted on the runways in the spring of 2003. Suddenly, the bags—not yet available in stores—graced the arm of nearly every Hollywood celebrity, including Paris Hilton, Jessica Simpson, and Lindsay Lohan.

Single and working in a lucrative career, I (Rebecca) drove myself to the Galleria Dallas, found the Louis Vuitton store, and placed my name on the waiting list. Shortly after, a girlfriend suggested that I try eBay. Many celebrities, she said, would carry a purse until the paparazzi snapped them with it, then sell it online.

To my delight, I found one nearly right away, complete with the dust bag, original tags, and a certificate of authenticity. I paid the price and awaited my purchase. Ten days later it arrived in all its glory. I carried my new purse everywhere, delighted by the squeals of envy it prompted from friends and strangers alike.

The same pal who tipped me off to eBay offered another piece of advice: "If you take it to the Louis store and register it, they'll clean it for you for life." I strode again through the arched doors of the luxury retailer, my white Takashi Murakami X Papillon bag tucked snuggly under my arm. I set it on the counter and smiled.

"What's this?" asked the clerk.

I explained that I had purchased the purse online and wanted to register it so I could have it cleaned.

"That's a fake purse," she said.

"What? No, it's not; I have a certificate of authenticity. I have the tags."

"Look," she replied and showed me the stitching. "That's obviously not a Louis. And look at this." She opened a catalog and showed me a picture. "See the difference in the monogram colors?"

She looked me square in the eyes and drove her point home. "What you have is a really bad fake. I hope you didn't pay too much for it." Stunned and humiliated, I turned and left.

My problem with Louis Vuitton purses was the same as the new believers in the churches of first-century Ephesus had. I didn't know the real thing well enough to recognize the wrong thing. The clerk at Louis Vuitton hadn't studied every counterfeit bag in existence. She didn't have to. She had enough experience with the real thing to know a fake when she saw it.

I never carried that purse again. Partly because I was embarrassed. But also because I knew that counterfeiters cost artists and designers millions of dollars in lost sales every year. To counterfeit is to deceive. Similarly, deceivers—counterfeiters of the truth—had made their way into Ephesus and were corrupting the pure teaching of the gospel and leading the believers in Timothy's charge astray.

Deceivers live among us, too, and we can recognize them when we study God's Word. Together, as we work our way through Paul's first letter to "his true son in the faith," we will soak ourselves in the truth and fortify ourselves against false teachings.

## ABOUT 1 TIMOTHY

First Timothy belongs to a small group of letters also containing 2 Timothy and Titus. All attributed to the apostle Paul, they differ significantly from his other writings in style and structure. Many scholars agree that the letters come from an aged pastor toward the end of his life after years spent toiling for the sake of the gospel on the mission field. Rather than treatises of doctrine written to multiple churches, these letters are personal correspondences to Paul's cherished co-workers as he transferred the cloak of ministry from his shoulders to theirs. Each epistle contains words of affirmation, exhortation, and caution.

Paul most likely wrote 1 Timothy in the mid-60s AD during a possible second Roman imprisonment. He had left Timothy, his dearest companion, in Ephesus to oversee the churches upon his departure for further church-planting work in Macedonia. Bible scholars consider Ephesus one of the most important geographical areas in Paul's time. Emperor Augustus honored the city as the capital of the province of Asia around 29 BCE.[2] Inscriptions call it "the first and greatest metropolis of Asia."[3] Known for the wealth and prosperity of its citizens, the city boasted a population of approximately 200,000 to 250,000 inhabitants.[4] Clearly, Ephesus presented an ideal location for carrying forth the gospel.

Evangelizing, however, was not without challenges. Anyone refusing to honor the emperor as lord and savior could face severe social and financial repercussions. Also, Ephesus housed the temple of Artemis, the virgin goddess of midwifery and protector of Ephesian citizens.[5] Some followers of the female-led cult practiced strict piety and self-denial, and

Clinton Arnold writes that many of the Ephesians were "new Christians in Asia Minor who turned to Christ from a background of devotion to the mother goddess Artemis and engaging in magic, witchcraft, and occultic practices. An understanding of the actual life-setting of the letter helps the reader to appreciate in a more profound way all that the Apostle Paul says about the Lord Jesus Christ and spiritual warfare."[1]

Emperor worship was strictly political. Honoring Roman rulers offered no protection or safeguard from the threatening evil "powers." Those seeking genuine religious experiences such as salvation, healing, or advice would need to seek it elsewhere.

Luke implies that a substantial number practiced magic (Acts 19), which followed many new believers into the church. This seaport swarmed with sailors, traders, soothsayers, and sellers of charms. Ephesus also hosted a substantial Jewish population, and the false teaching Paul warns about may have been a blend of Jewish and occult traditions.

While not an instruction manual for church structure, 1 Timothy offers invaluable insight concerning the qualities necessary for those who wish to serve as leaders. Paul's message is clear—character matters in the household of God.

Our culture is similar to Ephesus in some ways. Sincere believers trying to win souls to the faith find themselves fighting strange philosophies, new twists on ancient truth, and some "influencers" who lack integrity and credibility. Our character and conduct must honor Christ. Paul's words in 1 Timothy remain relevant to us today, for God and his Word remain the same forever (Psalm 102:27).

Of all ancient Greco-Roman cities, Ephesus, the third largest city in the Empire, was by far the most hospitable to magicians, sorcerers, and charlatans of all sorts.[6]

# Creating Beauty Out of Chaos | LESSON 1

Chaos—a jumbled feeling of utter confusion and disorder. We are living through an era shift, moving from a print to a technological age, and the result is cultural chaos. It feels a bit like anticipating the next aftershock of an earthquake, like straddling a massive crack in the earth that continues to expand. Not since the time of Johannes Gutenberg and the printing press some six hundred years ago has the Western world experienced such dramatic changes so rapidly. The ways we communicate, learn, relate, think, and worship have all changed. Barely any facet of our world today remains untouched. Scour the internet for information on how people are coping, and you'll see that anxiety is on the rise, especially among women and young people. One writer describes the cultural chaos we are experiencing this way:

> The product is an activity center where the inputs are hard to identify and the outputs are strange hydra headed Frankenstein beasts. No proof of provenance [origin] is available, no fact checking is done, no critical thought is applied. Theses [theory] monsters are built to get big fast, garner attention, and then deflate to nothingness . . . in a few days. This is not a problem if one's goal is to be entertained. This is a major hurdle if the goal is to problem solve.[1]

It's easy to be gobbled up in the turmoil of the times. We Christians must hang on to the sturdy cord of God's Word to lift us up and out of the chaos and set our feet on solid ground. God ordained that you would live during this era shift, and he desires that your life would be characterized by spiritual strength instead of confusion. Diamonds shine brightest against a dark background, so grab your Bible, get with others who also need God's lifeline, and ask the Lord to help you flourish despite the challenges. He can enable us all to create beauty out of the chaos.

OPTIONAL

**Memorize Isaiah 61:3**
[God will] bestow on them a crown of beauty instead of ashes, the oil of joy instead of mourning, and a garment of praise instead of a spirit of despair. They will be called oaks of righteousness, a planting of the LORD for the display of his splendor.

If you plan a trip to Singapore, you must learn about their customs and perspectives on life to truly enjoy and benefit from your travels. Before you can truly understand a book of the Bible, you must discover what life was like at that time.

Imagine you are a woman living in Ephesus two thousand years ago. Yes, her life was dramatically different in some ways, but it was much like yours in others. What lessons can you glean from Paul's letter to Timothy that can benefit Christian women of any century? That's the focus of our study. However, our saga begins before this letter. To understand it well, we must first travel back to Ephesus in the book of Acts.

## ❊ Read Acts 19:1–20.

When Paul arrived in Ephesus, he encountered people who had only heard a little about Jesus but who had experienced John's baptism of repentance. When Paul recognized they were deficient in their understanding of the Christian faith, he enlightened them and baptized them in the name of Jesus. Afterward, he followed his usual pattern of preaching to the city, first in the Jewish synagogue and later to the Gentiles, in the lecture hall of Tyrannus. This gathering place was available for traveling teachers from 11 a.m. to 4 p.m., when people met daily to eat their lunch and discuss the latest philosophies and ideas.

1. How far-reaching was Paul's two-year-long ministry of evangelistic preaching and conversations about Jesus (v. 10)?

2. What did God do through Paul to help the sick and oppressed (vv. 11–12)? As a result, what counterfeit activity began (v. 13)?

Paul taught between the hours of 11 a.m. and 4 p.m., during the siesta hours when others would rest and classes were not typically scheduled. In teaching through the heat of the day, Paul showed resourcefulness to use what was available to him and diligence to work during what in his culture was a time of relaxation. His commitment reminds us of Bible study leaders who teach in the evenings or pastors who work hard on Sunday mornings. When has fulfilling your calling required endurance to go above and beyond?

## DIGGING DEEPER

What are some ways you can discern counterfeit activities from authentic works of God?

3. What did the demons say to the seven sons of Sceva when they tried to imitate Paul (v. 15)? Then what did the demons do (v. 16)?

4. How did this event stop these fraudulent attempts to counterfeit authentic miracles (v. 17)?

How did the Ephesians who had been dabbling in the occult exhibit repentance (vv. 18–19)?

5. What kinds of magic arts and occult practices are becoming more widespread in your culture today? Why do you think some women are attracted? What are the dangers?

6. Did you or were you ever tempted to dabble in magic and occult practices? If so, what did you learn and how would you advise others who are curious?

The overriding characteristic of the practice of magic throughout the Hellenistic world was the cognizance of a spiritual world exercising influence over virtually every aspect of life. The goal of the magician was to discern the helpful spirits from the harmful ones and learn the distinct operations and the relative strengths and authority of the spirits. Through this knowledge, means could be constructed (with spoken or written formulas, amulets, etc.) for the manipulation of the spirits in the interest of the individual person. With the proper formula, a spirit-induced sickness could be cured, a chariot race could be won, sexual passions could be enhanced, etc. Conversely, great harm could be brought to another person through the utterance of a curse.[2]
—Clinton Arnold

### DIGGING DEEPER

Why do you think God chose to use extraordinary means to cure diseases and perform exorcisms in Ephesus? Why does God do this today in particular places around the world?

Witch culture turns its attention outward toward the System it aims to bring down. It is anti-institutional not merely in practice—modern witches cobble together a personal pantheon spanning several cultures and symbolic systems—but in its theology. Combining progressive feminist politics with a fervent opposition to institutional Christianity—which is dismissed and derided as a bastion of toxic patriarchy, repression, and white supremacy—modern witchcraft embraces its power to transgress.[3]
—Tara Isabella Burton

7. What are practices or habits from your old life that you (literally or metaphorically) may need to "burn" to experience freedom?

8. As believers were cleansed of these abominable practices, how was Paul's ministry affected (v. 20)? In your opinion, why? What are some practical applications for us today?

## 🌸 Read Acts 19:23–34.

Right before Paul planned to leave Ephesus, his ministry and Ephesian believers faced another potential death blow.

9. What charges did Demetrius bring against Paul? What do you think was the underlying reason he and the other silversmiths were actually outraged? (vv. 23–27)

For God is not the author of confusion but of peace.
—1 Corinthians 14:33 (NKJV)

10. What did you learn about Artemis of the Ephesians from the introduction to this study (see pages 14–15) that helps you understand her hold on the city and that part of the world?

11. Describe the chaos that ensued (vv. 28–34).

12. Why do you think the crowd lost control and began to shout and riot in the streets? How can we be sure we don't add to this kind of confusion and commotion when we are angry or frustrated? How do we help others when they are tempted to lose control and react foolishly?

Cooler heads prevailed when the city clerk reasoned with the mob, allowing Paul to escape and continue his missionary journeys (19:35–20:1). However, the church in Ephesus continued to be influenced by the Ephesian culture in Paul's absence. As a result, Paul sent Timothy as an ambassador to address issues within the church that were causing all kinds of chaos. He wrote the letter we'll be excavating to encourage and advise his mentee in the difficult task of cleansing an unhealthy church that had allowed outside influences to distort the true gospel. Many Christian communities struggle with the same toxic forces today, making these letters particularly profitable for us. Let's dig in.

## Read 1 Timothy 1:1–11.

13. According to verses 3 and 4, what has happened in the Ephesian church since Paul left? What does Paul urge Timothy to do as a result? What then is the first and primary reason Paul wrote this letter?

DIGGING DEEPER

Compare the salutations in these three personal letters to Timothy and Titus (1 Timothy 1:1-2; 2 Timothy 1:1-2; Titus 1:1-4). What does Paul emphasize in all three greetings? Contrast the salutations in his letter to Philemon (vv. 1-2) and Philippians (1:1-2). Why do you think Paul identifies himself differently in these letters?

14. Paul accuses the false teachers of forgetting "God's work—which is by faith" (v. 4). What should result from following the gospel that Paul taught (v. 5)? What does this tell you about the false doctrine that was being circulated in the Ephesian church?

15. What are the aspirations of the people circulating these false ideas (vv. 6–7)?

**DIGGING DEEPER**

Those who desire positions of authority and influence within the church would do well to consider James 3:1 and Matthew 20:25–28. What did Jesus advise those who desire to teach and lead to take to heart?

16. Have you ever witnessed a situation where someone wanted a highly regarded position, but they were not prepared for it? Why is it dangerous to give these people a place of influence before they are ready? What kinds of problems can these unhealthy aspirations create?

17. What kinds of words might be included in "meaningless talk" (v. 6)? Have you ever engaged in or been tempted to engage in this kind of rhetoric? How can you protect yourself from communicating this way?

In verses 8–10 Paul says that "the law is good if one uses it properly," but the false teachers are not. Therefore, the Ephesians should listen to Paul and Timothy. Greek scholar William D. Mounce writes,

The opponents have misunderstood the law. They are probably saying that Paul did not think the law was good. Vv 8–10 assert that the law is good but it must be used as it was intended. . . . Those who are righteous in Christ live according to a principle entirely different from the Mosaic law. Their righteous conduct is the outward expression of an inner transformation brought about by the indwelling presence of God. The opponents' misunderstanding of the law's function has led to spiritual sickness. Paul's gospel, on the other hand, brings spiritual health revealing God's wondrous glory.[5]

18. What has God done for Paul (v. 12)? Has God done the same for you? Are you living in light of this truth? Why or why not?

19. In verses 13–16 Paul weaved together his own personal history, the gospel in a nutshell, and advice to loyal Ephesian Christians on how to treat those who were naive and coming under the influence of the circulating heresies. List whatever lessons you can extrapolate from the verses:

Paul's personal history

The true gospel

Advice on how to treat those who act in ignorance

Much controversy surrounds "the law" (see vv. 7–10), which confirms that part of the problem surrounds misunderstanding, distortion, and misappropriation of Old Testament teaching and lore thrown in (note genealogies in v. 4), apparently with an admixture of Greco-Roman views (note "myths" v. 4). Such an amalgam would not be surprising at a cultural crossroads like Ephesus.[6]
—Robert Yarbrough

The Mosaic law has been done away in its entirety as a code. God is no longer guiding the life of man by this particular code. In its place He has introduced the law of Christ. Many of the individual commands within that law are new, but some are not. Some of the ones which are old were also found in the Mosaic law and they are now incorporated into the law of Christ. As a part of the Mosaic law they are completely and forever done away. As part of the law of Christ they are binding on the believer today.[7]
—Charles Ryrie

Christ is the culmination of the law so that there may be righteousness for everyone who believes.
—Paul (Romans 10:4)

I (Sue) knew very little about the Christian faith growing up and, as a result, dabbled in my early years in a variety of philosophies attempting to answer the big questions in life: Who am I? Why am I here? Where am I going? My parents believed children should be allowed to determine these answers for themselves. My husband was raised in a Christian home, although he abandoned those beliefs in college. After we were married and had children, I was invited to a women's Bible study where my search began in earnest. About the same time, we began to search for these kinds of answers as a couple. We were invited to join with a group of believers for informal discussions about life and God. No question was off-limits. And I had plenty! But through their kindness, patience, and thorough understanding of the Bible, I found answers that resulted in a joyous, intimate relationship with Christ and a transformed life. Never hesitate to ask your questions. God doesn't tell us everything, but he does tell us what we need to know to follow him wholeheartedly. Ask away.

20. In verse 13 Paul confesses that he was guilty of some of the sins he listed in verses 8–10. In your opinion, why did he list them? What does this reveal about God's love for sinful people? What are the lessons for us?

21. Paul ends his introductory portion of this letter with the first of three doxologies or hymns of praise (v. 17). Why do you think Paul bursts into praise following verses 12–16?

22. As you consider what Christ has done for you, what words of praise come to mind? Can you think of any roadblocks that hinder you from praising God wholeheartedly? If so, ask God why and consider discussing this with your group or a trusted Christian friend.

23. Paul renews his charge to Timothy to be bold and courageous while exhibiting tough love and to stand up to people instilling heretical beliefs in others (v. 18). He names two such people and explains that he "handed [them] over to Satan to be taught not to blaspheme" (v. 20). What do you think this means? Why do you think Paul did this?

24. Paul mentions Hymenaeus again in 2 Timothy 2:16–18, along with another false teacher named Philetus. How does Paul describe their heresies? What will be the results for both the heretics and those who come under their influence? Why is it imperative that we graciously but firmly confront teaching that distorts the essence of the true gospel?

25. What distortions, myths, and controversial speculations have you observed infiltrating the church today and resulting in confusion and chaos? (Please don't mention specific people, churches, political persuasions, or denominations.) What have you learned in this lesson that might help you be part of the solution to return to the true gospel?

26. Review the lesson. What did you learn that empowers you to create beauty out of chaos in your own life?

## BEAUTY OUT OF GARBAGE

Aside from Jesus, Paul is my favorite character in the New Testament, primarily because I (Rebecca) identify with him. At twelve years old, I began to suffer from severe generalized anxiety. As a result, I started drinking in middle school. My self-medicating habit had turned into alcoholism by the time I graduated college. I took my last drink in 2009, but I have plenty of shame-filled memories I'd like to erase.

One day, while working in my backyard, I noticed a plant growing out of my compost heap. An avocado pit had rooted and started to grow. I thought about it all day long, marveling over how God could produce life and beauty out of garbage.

That's when it hit me—God can create beauty from the garbage of our lives, too, when we entrust our lives to him.

# From Chaos to Tranquility | LESSON 2

Tranquility in a Christian's life is the sweet, gracious inward work of the Holy Spirit. It's the internal state of our hearts and minds holding their peace. It's a serene calm despite what's happening in our outer worlds. Is your life more characterized by chaos than tranquility? If so, you're missing one of the most precious perks of knowing Christ intimately.

Tourists travel from all over the world to drive the Pacific Coast Highway, stretching from Washington to California. From the comfort of your car, you are privy to the picturesque Pacific coast with cliffs, sea stacks, and the raging ocean. Mammoth waves catapult fifty feet in the air, pounding and thrashing—but if you go fifty feet below the surface, you'll experience the calm and quiet of the ocean bed.

Living in this fallen world is like living on the sea's surface, where you never know when one of those enormous waves will drench you. But in lesson 2, Paul shows us how to escape the anxiety that easily results from life's turmoil and frenzy. He carries us to the white sands of the ocean floor where brilliantly colored sea creatures and green flora silently glide and gently sway, a waveless place of peace. A tranquil life is the Holy Spirit's glorious gift, but you must choose it over chaos.

## ❧ Read 1 Timothy 2:1–7.

Prayer is our first practice to combat chaos in our own personal lives, in the Christian community, and in the secular culture.

1. Who does Paul instruct the Ephesians to pray for (v. 1)? Specifically, what does Paul instruct them to ask for (v. 2)? Why (vv. 3–6)?

OPTIONAL

**Memorize Isaiah 26:3–4**
You will keep in perfect peace those whose minds are steadfast, because they trust in you. Trust in the LORD forever, for the LORD, the LORD himself, is the Rock eternal.

From this point on in the letter, a number of specific issues will receive attention. The context throughout will continue to be that of false teaching and opposition to the Pauline mission. As Paul treats matters related to the worship gathering and the organization of leaders, and gives instructions concerning various groups, the church will often still feel the presence of opponents and their teaching activities.[1]
—Philip Towner

27

The word *quiet* related to all the people in 2:2 is the same word related to women's behavior in 2:11 and 12.

Try to keep your soul always in peace and quiet, always ready for whatever our Lord may wish to work in you.[2]
—Saint Ignatius

2. What do you think it means to live "a quiet life"? What does Paul say will result (1 Thessalonians 4:11–12)?

3. Does the culture where you live encourage people to live peaceful, quiet lives? What cultural norms and pressures usually work against this kind of serene existence?

4. Would you characterize your life right now as peaceful and quiet or full of confusion and chaos? Why? If the latter, what concrete steps can you take to eliminate the confusion and chaos and move toward more peace and quiet?

5. Paul seems to be connecting the idea of believers' living peaceful and quiet lives with God's desire that all people "be saved and to come to a knowledge of the truth" (1 Timothy 2:4). How might the first idea lead to the second?

6. What "knowledge" and "truth" does God the Father yearn for all people to understand (vv. 5–6)? What can you do to help God's desire be realized?

For you know that it was not with perishable things such as silver or gold that you were redeemed from the empty way of life handed down to you from your ancestors, but with the precious blood of Christ, a lamb without blemish or defect.
—1 Peter 1:18–19

7. In verse 7 Paul communicates his credentials to Timothy and the Ephesian church. Why do you think he needs to do this?

Reading a New Testament epistle can be a little like listening to only one side of a conversation. God has provided Paul's response for us in 1 and 2 Timothy, but we don't know all the precise details of what was going on in the Ephesian church that prompted Paul's response. For instance, as we read verse 8, it's important to remember that of course women should also pray, and we should also avoid anger and quarreling! Yet Paul directs this verse specifically to men because he is addressing a particular situation in Ephesus. —Sue

## Read 1 Timothy 2:8.

Next, Paul provides gender-specific instructions to men and then to women to lessen the chaos and confusion in Ephesus caused by disagreements and arguments over circulating heresies and false teaching.

8. What does Paul instruct the men to do? What attitudes does he insist they leave behind? (verse 8) What can you assume the Ephesian men have been doing in light of Paul's admonition? What dangers might result if this kind of behavior continues?

Men ancient and modern often relish disagreement. They love to be right and will go to great lengths to vindicate themselves and disparage real or perceived foes. Road-rage incidents, almost always involving men, offer contemporary illustration. Self-righteousness easily forgets and may effectively contradict the assertion that "the anger of man does not produce the righteousness of God" (Jas 1:20 ESV).[3]
—Robert Yarbrough

9. Have you witnessed men exhibiting this kind of behavior (no names, please)? If so, what damage resulted?

Next Paul instructs Timothy regarding women's behavior that has been creating confusion and chaos in Ephesus. First Timothy 2:9–15 is one of the most difficult and disputed passages in the whole Bible. Attempt to see this text as if for the first time. We will work through these verses line by line in this lesson and the next. We will give you an opportunity to discern what you think Paul is advising Timothy concerning women in Ephesus. Then you must decide whether Paul meant for his instructions to apply only to women in Ephesus or to the church for all time. Discuss respectfully and with an irenic spirit.

## ❃ Read 1 Timothy 2:9–10.

10. Paul points out three areas where some of the women are inappropriate according to first-century Roman customs. What are they (v. 9)? What seems to be Paul's first concern regarding the women at Ephesus?

### What Communicated Godly Beauty in the First-Century Roman Empire?

> The extensive evidence from portraiture, frescos, sculpture, and vase paintings in Greek and Roman cities of Paul's day almost universally depicts respectable women with their hair done up.[5]

Most artifacts of Paul's day don't show women wearing veils or any covering over their heads. Instead, they wore their hair in all sorts of elaborate and even ostentatious massive beehives and ornate patterns, requiring lengthy grooming sessions. It's likely some Christian women were imitating these extreme fashions, as some women do today, and Paul expressed concern. But neither was Paul instructing women to wear their hair down, loose, and wild.

> For women to have loose hair in public, however, was conventionally seen as shameful; a sign associated either with prostitutes or—perhaps worse from Paul's point of view—with women caught up in ecstatic worship practices of cults associated with Dionysius, Cybele, and Isis.[6]

Glahn suggests,

> Most likely the wives were "letting down their hair," a practice probably associated with spiritual freedom in Dionysus worship.

But doing so was the equivalent to taking off their wedding rings, which shamed their husbands and suggested they were "available."[7]

If women were not to wear their hair loose and not to imitate the ostentatious styles of done-up hair that worldly women were wearing, what was Paul asking godly women to do? Bruce Winter writes,

> Statue types displayed the simple hairstyles which epitomized the modest wife and were worn by members of the imperial family. These statues were replicated throughout the empire and represented "fashion icons" to be copied by modest married women.[8]

Paul is suggesting that a Christian woman wear her hair neatly over her head, typically twisted and tied up with some sort of fastener, so as not to call undue attention to herself but instead to focus attention on Christ. Paul is concerned about what women's hairstyles would communicate to a watching world.

11. If Paul were evaluating women in your culture, what might he point out as inappropriate for a godly Christian woman today? What deep needs do you think motivate women obsessed with appearance?

12. Instead of focusing on an unhealthy obsession with bodily appearance, where does Paul advise Christian women to spend their energy (v. 10)? What struggles and tensions surface in your life as you hear this admonition?

The LORD does not look at the things people look at. People look at the outward appearance, but the LORD looks at the heart.
—1 Samuel 16:7

13. How are we in the twenty-first century tempted to flaunt our wealth or rank in our purchases, lifestyle choices, or clothing? What would it look like for you to adorn yourself with good works instead?

❀ Read 1 Timothy 2:11.

14. What is Paul encouraging women to do in the first part of verse 11?

15. Why do you think this command might be important for women in the first century and throughout history?

16. What is a learning opportunity you have treasured in your own life?

17. Paul is referring not to outward silence but to an inward heart attitude. What attitude does Paul say is appropriate for Ephesian women when they are learning? Why do you think this heart attitude pleases not only teachers but also God?

18. What does Paul's command suggest might be going on among the women at Ephesus?

19. How are you following Paul's mandate to learn in verse 11 in your life today? What concrete step could you take to grow in this area?

20. What does a quiet spirit look like in your life?

DIGGING DEEPER

The Greek word translated as *quietness* in 1 Timothy 2:11 is also used in 2 Thessalonians 3:12; 1 Timothy 2:2; and 1 Peter 3:4. What other ideas about quietness are contained in these verses?

21. Paul also says that women should learn in "full submission" (verse 11). What do you think this means? If you have been a professional teacher, what can you add to the discussion?

In marriage, wives and husbands are asked to submit to one another. Then wives are instructed to submit to their husbands and husbands to sacrifice for their wives (Ephesians 5:21–33). Submission means coming under another to support and encourage them, sometimes giving up one's preferences when it's in the best interest of the other. Sacrificial love has similar connotations. As both partners attempt to out-submit and out-sacrifice one another, their marriage can blossom with health and reciprocal love and respect.

22. Discuss what the following passages reveal about submission.

James 3:17

James 4:7

Do an in-depth study of the concept of submission in the Bible. In what key areas of life does God ask all believers to live with a submissive attitude? What does this word mean in Greek? There are a variety of views in Christian literature today. Read about these views. Which do you hold and why?

Study Ephesians 5:21–33 carefully, especially the terms *submit* and *sacrifice*. Why do you think Paul asks wives to submit to their husbands and husbands to sacrifice for their wives? Compare and contrast these two concepts.

"Blessed are the single-hearted, for they shall enjoy much peace." . . . If you refuse to be hurried and pressed, if you stay your soul on God, nothing can keep you from that clearness of spirit which is life and peace. In that stillness you will know what His will is.[9]
—Amy Carmichael, missionary to India

1 Peter 5:5—6

1 Corinthians 16:15–16

23. What have you learned in this lesson that would help reduce chaos in your life and replace it with tranquility and peace?

## RUN WITH THE WIND

I (Rebecca) come from a family of marathoners. Although injuries prevented me from running the two 26.3-mile races I'd trained for, I've loved long-distance running for over thirty years. Today my runs rarely surpass four miles, but lacing up my shoes and pounding the pavement remains my favorite way to decompress. I often use the time to pray and listen for God's voice.

I live in north Texas, a region known for high winds throughout the spring. Pushing through a strong gust makes running difficult, even when you're going downhill. Likewise, even an uphill climb requires little exertion when you have the wind at your back.

So it is with the Holy Spirit. I have found that when I submit myself to God's will, I have peace, even when life leads me through deep valleys. But when I try to force my will or way, it's like running against the wind—far more difficult than it should be and devoid of peace. When we surrender to God's still, small voice, we run in step with the wind of the Spirit.

# Gender Chaos—What's a Woman to Do?

Imagine the following scenario.

Taylor and Morgan, a married couple with teens, lead the college ministry at their church. On any given Sunday evening, Taylor and Morgan have cooked food and cleaned their home in preparation for the group, who enjoy conversation and food before transitioning to teaching time. Taylor strums a worship song on the guitar, then opens with prayer. Finally, Morgan walks up and says, "Let's open our Bibles" to begin teaching the lesson.

Depending on your understanding of the Bible's teaching on leadership, you may have instinctively identified Morgan as the husband in the couple. But does it have to be? Can Taylor be the husband who takes the supporting role while his wife, Morgan, teaches the lesson?

That God gifts women and men alike with various skills, talents, and abilities has never been in question. Where, when, and how a woman uses her gifts in line with the Bible's instruction remains a disputed issue.[1]

No one talking about what Christian women can do can get around 1 Timothy 2:11–12. When my (Sue's) students raise their hands to ask a question concerning women in ministry, often it's about understanding this text. Some feel compelled to comply with what they believe is the "plain reading" of Scripture. Others insist that, in contrast, it's necessary to go beyond surface appearances. Godly, sincere people come to different conclusions, although all admit the passage includes some of the most confounding phrases in Scripture.

Yes, 1 Timothy 2 is a challenging passage. So how should we approach it in our Bible study? We might be tempted to avoid it altogether, but we can approach this chapter trusting that all Scripture is profitable and worth any extra effort required to understand it. We can also approach this chapter trusting that God is kind and that his plan for men and women is good. What wise insights can we find in this chapter to apply to our lives?

1. What assumptions did you grow up with concerning women and their "place" in the family and church (no names or denominations, please)?

2. Have you changed any of your views related to women and if so, why?

3. Why do you think the role of women is such a divisive issue today?

4. Through the centuries many women have suffered from sexism and prejudice. What do the following verses reveal about women's value and purpose?

   Genesis 1:26–28

   1 Peter 2:9–10

   Matthew 28:18–20

🌸 **Read 1 Timothy 2:12 and digest the various perspectives in the note that follows.**

Multiple scholars have spilled seas of ink and worked late into the night in their passion to figure out what Paul meant when he wrote this verse to Timothy. Before we attempt to discern the possible interpretations, we need to answer the question below. We will attempt to provide the various views fairly.

### What Is the Meaning and Significance of the Greek Word Authentein?

The English translation of this term is "authority." In the whole Bible, the only place *authentein* is used for the idea of authority is in 1 Timothy 2:12. Some scholars point out that Paul could have easily used the other more common term for authority, *exousia*, which communicates the idea of giving permission, the right, the liberty, or the power to do something and appears over and over throughout the New Testament. They ask why Paul would choose the rare term *authentein* if he meant the same sort of authority that *exousia* would have communicated.

Scholars also disagree on whether the term *authentein*:

- denotes a negative meaning—a term a writer might use to condemn a practice done that way; or
- denotes a neutral meaning—a term a writer might use that communicates a fact without implying whether it's recommended or discouraged.

Greek dictionaries offer these definitions of *authenté*, the root word of *authentein*.

- To control in a domineering manner[2] (negative)
- To have full power over[3] (neutral)
- One who acts on his own authority; domineer, lord it over[4] (negative)
- Give orders to[5] (neutral)
- Domineer, have authority over[6] (negative)
- One who with his own hands kills another or himself; one who acts on his own authority, autocratic; an absolute master; to govern, exercise dominion over one[7]

I grew up in the 1980s and '90s in a Christian context that was in a pendulum-swing reaction to second-wave feminism. Biblical passages like 1 Timothy 2 were used to teach me that women were inferior and that I would be wrong to seek an education or job or any purpose beyond being a wife and mother. In my twenties and early thirties, I wrestled with how God and his Word was really for me as a woman. I've come to stand on the truth that "the LORD is righteous in all his ways and faithful in all he does" (Psalm 145:17). I can trust that God is good and that he is for me as a woman. The Bible gives me equal value and purpose as one created in the image of God (Genesis 1:26–28) and a co-heir of God's grace (1 Peter 3:7). My primary identity, no matter what my role or season in life, is in being a disciple of Christ. Extrabiblical rules lead to legalism and bondage, but truth sets us free (John 8:32). Now I can say with the psalmist, "I run in the path of your commands, for you have broadened my understanding" (Psalm 119:32).

—Lisa Adams

For a more thorough treatment of these issues, see Edwards and Mathews, *40 Questions About Women in Ministry*, questions 23, 24, and 25.

If you choose to translate *authentein* in a more neutral sense, you imply that Paul uses the word to mean that he never permits a woman to "exercise authority" over a man. Then you would limit women from all kinds of authority over men for all time.

If you choose to translate *authentein* in a more negative sense, you imply that Paul was correcting women from teaching in a domineering or abusive way—not prohibiting them from all teaching and authority.

Also, some claim it's impossible to glean a clear understanding of the term *authentein* and all these confusing passages unless we consider the cultural context, especially related to Ephesian women and the likelihood that many of them had recently come out of a lifetime in the Artemis cult before they accepted Christ. Current research indicates that women had the opportunity to oversee ceremonies and lead in the Great Temple in Ephesus, and that wealthy women in the city were pushing back on the gender limitations typical of the first century, like we are experiencing today.

Others believe that these ideas are wishful thinking. These views are an attempt to accommodate the culture—a culture today where women have more opportunities to teach and lead in the secular culture than they do in the church. They insist that this text clearly states that women are never to teach Christian doctrine to men nor are they ever to exercise authority directly over men in the church. These restrictions are permanent and authoritative for the church for all time. Some who hold this view make exceptions; for example, they allow women to teach a mixed gender Sunday school class or small group but never to "preach" to the whole congregation. Others don't allow women to "preach," but they can give a testimony or a mission's report.

DIGGING DEEPER

After listening to others, doing additional study, and taking more time to consider all sides of this controversial issue, write an essay on what you believe is the meaning of 1 Timothy 2:12.

---

❧

---

5. After carefully reading and analyzing "What Is the Meaning and Significance of the Greek Word *Authentein*?," what are your thoughts? Does understanding more about the meaning of *authentein* affect your perspective on this verse? If so, why? If not, why not? What ideas do you find most compelling? Discuss kindly and respectfully.

❋ Read 1 Timothy 2:13 and digest the various perspectives in the note that follows.

### What Is the Significance that Adam Was Created First and Eve Second?

For centuries, scholars understood these verses to mean that women were not to teach men because they were intellectually inferior to men.

William Witt writes,

> Women were considered less rational, more gullible, and more susceptible to temptation, and thus were restricted not only from church office, but from any position of authority over men whatsoever.[8]

Today's scholars have largely abandoned inferiority as a reason that women cannot teach men, acknowledging that women are no more gullible or less intelligent than men.

Instead, some point to Genesis 2—creation order. Because Paul grounded his argument in 1 Timothy 2 in creation, a universal truth, he was speaking of all women in a universal sense when he told Timothy that they could not teach men. Thus, women cannot teach men because they were created after them. They contend that this view is the clear teaching of the text and provides a pattern that should be followed when interpreting the rest of the Bible. They insist that this teaching falls in line with the authority patterns taught elsewhere in the Bible and must be followed to maintain the order that God desires in the world.

However, other scholars discount this idea because they insist that much of Scripture turns the idea of automatic favor of the first on its head. Examples they cite include:

A. *Jacob and Esau.* In Genesis 25, Isaac's wife Rebecca was pregnant with twin boys. Before she gave birth, the Lord told her, "Two nations are in your womb, and two peoples from within you will be separated; one people will be stronger than the other, and the older will serve the younger" (v. 23). This prophecy came to fruition in the lives of Jacob and Esau, with Jacob, the younger, receiving God's favor as the son of the covenant and whose children became Israel, God's chosen people.

B. *The Choosing of King David.* When God instructed Samuel to find and anoint the next king (1 Samuel 16), David's father brought Samuel his sons, all except the youngest, assuming that Samuel would choose from the older boys. But God didn't affirm any of the seven older sons; instead, God said to Samuel,

And first, where that I affirm the empire of a woman to be a thing repugnant to nature, I mean not only that God by the order of his creation has spoiled woman of authority and dominion, but also that man has seen, proved and pronounced just causes why that it so should be. . . . For who can deny but it is repugnant to nature, that the blind shall be appointed to lead and conduct such as do see? That the weak, the sick, and impotent persons shall nourish and keep the whole and strong, and finally, that the foolish, mad and frantic shall govern the discrete, and give counsel to such as be sober of mind? And such be all women, compared to man in bearing of authority.[9]
—John Knox (1514–1572)

Wayne Grudem writes, "Adam was created first, was put in the garden and given commands by God, and Eve was created as a helper for Adam; in that sequence of events God gave to Adam a leadership role."[10] Grudem goes on to argue that in the Hebrew family and in much of the ancient world, everyone would have understood this, and this pattern preserves a certain order, is for all time, and will result in God's best for everyone. Because Adam was first, he is logically the leader of the couple.

While Adam and Eve's relationship revolves around unity and love, it is also characterized by more than equality. At the same time, it lacks any explicit commands for Adam to exercise authority over Eve but does emphasize the obedience of both Adam and Eve to God. Whatever the nature of any authority Adam might have, it is not presented in a dominant fashion. Furthermore, it is difficult to see how authority would be a primary characteristic of Adam's role if one of his main duties is to create unity between the two.[11]
—Michelle Lee-Barnewall

Do not consider his appearance or his height, for I have rejected him. The LORD does not look at the things people look at. People look at the outward appearance, but the LORD looks at the heart. (v. 7)

Then Samuel asked the father to bring his youngest son from the fields. When young David arrived, the Lord said to Samuel, "Rise and anoint him; this is the one" (v. 12).

C. *The Life and Teaching of Jesus.* When Jesus's disciples were arguing about who was the greatest among them, Jesus said to them, "Anyone who wants to be first must be the very last, and the servant of all" (Mark 9:35). Then he took a little child in his arms as an object lesson. Jesus was born into poverty. Many of the disciples were uneducated fishermen. They argue that Jesus didn't use cultural norms to measure God's best ways.

These scholars challenge Christians to decide whether being first reflects the tone of who God is, his attributes, his character, and what he values most. They acknowledge that men and women are different, but they contend that the "order of creation" argument to put males in a permanent leadership role in the family, church, and community is not in sync with the overall tone of the Scriptures and who God is.

Also, they do not accept the idea that creation order in Genesis 1 and 2 implies that birth order gives men authority over women, but instead they insist that these passages describe the mutual callings, oneness, and divine image bearing of men and women.

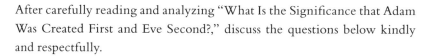

After carefully reading and analyzing "What Is the Significance that Adam Was Created First and Eve Second?," discuss the questions below kindly and respectfully.

6. What do you think is the "big idea" of Genesis 1 and 2 related to the roles of men and women?

7. Which idea do you find most compelling: *birth order* or *the first will be last* when interpreting 1 Timothy 2:13? Why?

Yet the reason Paul assigns, that woman was second in the order of creation, appears not to be a very strong argument in favour of her subjection; for John the Baptist was before Christ in the order of time, and yet was greatly inferior in rank.[12]
—John Calvin (1509–1564)

❋ Read 1 Timothy 2:14 and digest the various perspectives in the note that follows.

### Why Did Paul Point Out that Eve Was Easily Deceived and Caused the Fall?

Most scholars today refute the idea that women are primarily to blame for the fall and are more easily deceived, which they say verse 14 seems to imply on the surface but isn't supported by other biblical texts. They look to Romans 5:12–19:

> For if, by the trespass of the one man [Adam], death reigned through that one man, how much more will those who receive God's abundant provision of grace and of the gift of righteousness reign in life through the one man, Jesus Christ! (v. 17)

They argue that although Eve was deceived, Adam knowingly sinned against God, and both are equally accountable. In addition, men have proven to be just as easily deceived through the ages as women. And since Paul also wrote Romans 5 assigning blame for the fall on Adam, Paul must have meant something else in 1 Timothy 2:14. What could he have meant instead? The answer isn't clear, but below are some suggested possibilities:

A. Paul may be using the idea of Eve's deception as a local, temporary example.[13] Just like Eve was easily deceived since she didn't get the direct command not to eat the fruit like Adam did, these uneducated Ephesian women were especially susceptible to deception and temptation and therefore ill-prepared at that time to teach. "The point of the example [of Adam and Eve] is to teach women not to emulate Eve."[14]

B. Paul wrote verse 14 to counter pagan myths embraced by former Artemis worshippers who were now Christians. These women had been immersed in the pagan worship of the goddess Artemis and the related stories. Some were likely still influenced by their former "religion" and the worldly culture of the city where they lived. And because the primary deity they worshipped in Ephesus was a woman, they had an elevated view of the status of women over men. Clinton Arnold, in his extensive research on the Artemis cult, writes, "One undisputed characteristic of the Ephesian Artemis is the unsurpassed cosmic power attributed to her."[15]

C. Another idea relates to the mythological creation story of Artemis and her male twin Apollo. According to the legend, they were the children of Zeus, the king of all the other gods, and Leto, a Titan goddess. Artemis was a virgin, the mother of all life as creator, the guardian of young children, and the protector of women in labor. In contrast, Apollo was a male god with many lovers, and he was the one who brought sin into the world.[16] In the Artemis creation narrative, the woman came into the world before the man, exactly the opposite of the creation account in Genesis. As relatively new Christians, these women were desperately in need of learning sound Christian doctrine.

Even worse, some who had enjoyed the elevated status of women in the upper echelons of the pagan priesthood may have, out of ignorance, synthesized the two belief systems and were spreading their false ideas. This would account for Paul's continued rebuke of those who "want to be teachers of the law, but they do not know what they are talking about or what they so confidently affirm" (1:7). Paul was correcting these women, telling them to stop promoting these myths in the house of God. In 1 Timothy 4:7 Paul wrote, "But reject those myths fit only for the godless and gullible, and train yourself for godliness" (NET). The accompanying note by NET Bible scholars reads, "Those myths refer to the legendary tales characteristic of the false teachers in Ephesus and Crete."[17]

Having been immersed in Artemis worship, women who had converted to faith in Jesus could have imported old domineering habits into the church, insisting they be allowed to teach when they were not yet competent and demanding they be given unqualified authority. Paul was advising these women to remember that the first woman had been deceived just like they were being deceived.

D. All of this is speculation and a stretch. Andreas and Margaret Köstenberger write,

> In verses 13–14, Paul is simply reading the Genesis narrative and registering some basic observations. The Serpent approached the woman and deceived the woman, not the man. Why did the Serpent approach the woman when the man was in charge and had received both the direct

In these Gentiles' [Ephesians'] creation narrative, the woman came first, and that gave her preeminence as the first twin. Competition persisted between cities that worshiped one or the other of the twins, with Artemis's followers insisting she was superior because she was born first. So in Timothy's context, the creation story from Genesis contrasts completely with the local story and would have served as a logical corrective.[18]

—Sandra Glahn

mandate to cultivate the garden and the direct prohibition from God concerning the Tree of the Knowledge of Good and Evil? Paul reminds his readers what happened historically when the woman acted apart from the man, leading him into disobedience, rather than the man fulfilling his role and leading the woman.[19]

They believe this view is more straightforward and logical. Thomas Schreiner adds, "There is no clear evidence in Paul's letters that the Artemis cult played a role. Paul does not mention the cult, nor is there any specific notion in the text that shows the influence of the cult."[20]

---

❋

---

8. After carefully reading and analyzing "Why Did Paul Point Out that Eve Was Easily Deceived and Caused the Fall?," what are your thoughts related to the suggested possibilities? Discuss kindly and respectfully.

❋ Read 1 Timothy 2:15 and digest the various perspectives in the note that follows.

### What Did Paul Mean When He Wrote These Perplexing Words to Ephesian Women?

Verse 15 is notoriously difficult to interpret. Earlier Paul wrote, "For it is by grace you have been saved, through faith—and this is not from yourselves, it is the gift of God—not by works, so that no one can boast" (Ephesians 2:8–9). Obviously, women do not receive salvation by bearing children or even by proper behavior, which would be by works, but by accepting the undeserved gift of life through faith in what Christ did on the cross on their behalf. So, Paul must mean something else. Below are several options.

A. Paul was using the term *saved* in the sense of Philippians 2:12: "continue to work out your salvation with fear and trembling." Thus, verse 15 would apply to all women. Douglas Moo writes,

> We think it is preferable to view verse 15 as designating the circumstances in which Christian women will experience (work out; cf. Philippians 2:12) their salvation—in maintaining as priorities those key roles that Paul, in keeping with Scripture elsewhere, highlights: being faithful, helpful wives, raising children to love and reverence God, managing the household.[21]

B. Paul means *saved* in the sense of "to be kept safe." Andreas Köstenberger writes that most evangelicals hold that women will be spiritually preserved, or saved, if they devote themselves to their God-given role in the domestic and familial spheres.[22] Women who stray outside these realms put themselves in danger of "satanic deception" when they, like Eve, believe, "You can do better than abiding by God's design and submitting to the man."[23]

C. This verse should be understood as "*the* childbearing." Rather than having anything to do with Ephesian women bearing children, it's a reference to the birth of Christ, the promised Savior. In this sense, all women will be saved through Mary giving birth to Jesus when women place their faith in Christ—if they continue in faith, love, and holiness with propriety.[24]

D. It's only possible to glean a clear understanding of this confusing text by considering the cultural context, especially related to Ephesian women and the likelihood that many of them had recently come out of a lifetime in the Artemis cult before they accepted Christ. In ancient Rome, for example, rough (conservative) estimates suggest that there were 25 maternal deaths and 300 infant deaths, respectively, for every 1,000 live births.[25]

Obviously, Ephesian women feared dying while in labor. However, the goddess Artemis was believed to watch over and protect women during childbirth, but only those who were her loyal followers.

In this view the identity of the goddess provides a clearer explanation of why Paul would write that women will be "saved through childbearing—if they continue in faith, love and holiness with propriety" (v. 15). Christian women who came out of this cult where they believed they were protected by Artemis, the goddess of childbearing, might naturally be fearful that they were offending the goddess by leaving the cult. And they were especially in danger when giving birth. Paul is attempting to soothe their fears and encourage them to trust in God by persevering in "faith, love, and holiness" rather than returning to their old beliefs that would show they were still living in fear of the goddess.[28]

9. After carefully reading and analyzing "What Did Paul Mean When He Wrote These Perplexing Words to Ephesian Women?," what are your thoughts related to the suggested possibilities? Summarize your thoughts. What are key concepts, if any, that you believe the church should take away and apply? Discuss kindly and respectfully.

10. Almost all women in the first century experienced arranged marriages because, generally, women had no way to provide the necessities for themselves. What does Paul advise women without male assistance in 1 Corinthians 7:8, 17, and 23–24? What comfort might this give you if you are single or if you suffer from infertility? If you are a wife or mother, how can you encourage your friends in different situations?

11. We learned that childbirth was the primary cause of death in the first century and that Artemis was believed to be able to protect women in labor. Imagine you are a pregnant woman in first-century Ephesus. You used to worship Artemis to keep you safe in childbirth, but now you worship Jesus and are struggling with fear. How might 1 Timothy 2:15 comfort you?

12. Do you believe that God loves women just as much as men? Why or why not?

13. Why do you believe God created you as female?

DIGGING DEEPER

All Scripture must be interpreted in light of the whole Bible, and God never contradicts himself. Do a character study on one or all of the biblical women below. What did each woman do? What resulted? How can you harmonize this information with what you learned in this lesson?

Deborah (Judges 4–5)
Huldah (2 Chronicles 34:14–33)
Anna (Luke 2:36–38)
Priscilla (Acts 18:1–3, 18–19; Romans 16:3)

14. What do you believe is God's primary purpose for women? Are you fulfilling your purpose? Why or why not?

15. Prayerfully read Jesus's last prayer request before he went to the cross in John 17:20–23, where he prays first for his disciples and then for us. What was his final request? Why is this so important to Jesus? How might Jesus's request influence how we love those with different views on what men and women can do in the church and home?

## What To Do If You Find Yourself in Disagreement with the Leadership at Your Church

Remember that the role of women in the church is not a primary doctrine (like the Trinity or salvation). Mature, Bible-believing Christians respectfully disagree about this issue.

A good rule of Bible interpretation is to let passages that are clearer inform our application of passages that are less clear. You have probably realized by now that 1 Timothy 2 is not the clearest passage in the Bible! Passages that are clear include Ephesians 4:3 that says, "Make every effort to keep the unity of the Spirit through the bond of peace," and Hebrews 13:17:

> Have confidence in your leaders and submit to their authority, because they keep watch over you as those who must give an account. Do this so that their work will be a joy, not a burden, for that would be of no benefit to you.

Clothed with these attitudes, you may flourish in an environment where there may be disagreement about secondary doctrines. Of course, if you find yourself in a context that is spiritually harmful, seek wise counsel regarding where the best community for you might be to grow and to exercise your gifts to serve others.

**—Lisa Adams**

# Taking Action to Calm the Chaos

What comes to mind when you think of leaders? Perhaps you conjure up the image of the Oval Office or a CEO striding confidently down a hallway with a gaggle of mid-level managers struggling to keep up. Maybe you think of a mother herding her children through the grocery store or a teacher calling for order in the classroom.

You lead in some way no matter what you do or where you are in life. God gives each of us a circle of influence that travels with us wherever we go, whether in the home, at work, at the doctor's office, or at a homeowner's association meeting. Leaders influence people, and you have the opportunity to influence people for Jesus.

In chapter 2, Paul focused on the congregational behavior in Ephesus. In chapter 3, he shifts his attention to the character of godly leaders, an antidote to chaos and confusion. A literal translation of 1 Timothy 3:1 in Greek reads, "If one aspires to [be an] overseer, he/she desires good work." Those endowed with the spiritual gift of leadership should put their gifts to use for God's glory. However, this "good work" comes with great responsibility. Perhaps you have heard the saying, "What leaders do in moderation, their followers will do in excess." Because people tend to imitate those they admire, those entrusted with leadership positions must understand that society holds them to a higher standard.

Paul writes with two types of church leaders in mind—overseers and deacons. We will see, however, that all Christians can apply these principles to their lives as they seek to navigate their circles of influence with grace and integrity.

## Read 1 Timothy 3:1–7.

Today, different churches operate under various organizational structures. The first churches planted by the apostles seemed to operate with the first-century apostles in the highest leadership positions, with overseers (or elders) and deacons who ministered with them. As you read Paul's

---

**OPTIONAL**

**Memorize Luke 22:24–26**

A dispute also arose among them as to which of them was considered to be greatest. Jesus said to them, "The kings of the Gentiles lord it over them; and those who exercise authority over them call themselves Benefactors. But you are not to be like that. Instead, the greatest among you should be like the youngest, and the one who rules like the one who serves."

instructions, think about how these verses impact you as you operate in your circle of influence.

## INSTRUCTIONS FOR OVERSEERS

1. Verse 1 tells us that those who desire the position of overseer desire a good work, or, as the NIV phrases it, "a noble task." Knowing that you have a circle of influence, what does leadership look like in your life? Whom do you "oversee"? Who are the people you are influencing? How do you desire to impact them?

2. What is your definition of leadership? Have you ever considered yourself a leader? In your opinion, what makes a godly leader, and who qualifies as such?

3. First, Paul says a leader must be "above reproach" (v. 2). What do you think Paul means? Why is this important? What does this mean for you in your circle of influence?

4. Paul states nine additional qualifications for overseers in verses 2–3, listed on the next page from the NIV. Using your own words, write a short description for each term. You are free to use a dictionary for clarification. After you define the terms, pick several and write an example of how you can implement these characteristics in your own life.

Temperate


Self-controlled


Respectable


Hospitable


Able to teach


Not given to drunkenness


Gentle


Not quarrelsome


Not a lover of money

5. Look at your definitions from the previous page. Which of these come easily for you? Which needs improvement?

In verse 2, another qualification in Greek reads "one-wife husband." These words have presented translators with many challenges. Different views include:

- The overseer must abstain from polygamy.
- The overseer must not be divorced.
- The overseer could have only one wife ever. Since Paul, in other letters, allows widows to remarry (see 1 Timothy 5:14; Romans 7:2–3; 1 Corinthians 7:39), this is unlikely.
- The NIV's "faithful to one wife" seems best when understood to mean that a husband should take the covenant of marriage seriously, maintaining fidelity to his wife.

6. Have you attended a church that endured a minister's moral failure? How did that make you feel? How did the church respond? What happened in the aftermath? What does this say to a watching world (no names, please)?

**DIGGING DEEPER**

Read Ephesians 5:25–31. How did Paul describe a faithful husband? Why would these qualities be important in leading a ministry?

7. In 1 Timothy 3:4, Paul writes that overseers must manage their families well. The idea of managing comes from the Greek word *proistēmi*, which can mean to "show concern for, care for" or "to exercise a position of leadership."[1] Skim back over verses 1–3 and then write out what you believe Paul desires from leaders when he speaks of a well-managed family.

8. Based on your previous answer, what are some practices you can implement to ensure a peace-filled household? If you are single, what can you do to see that you are leading in a way that leads to peace in your circle of influence?

9. In verse 4, Paul seems to be focusing on the way leaders interact with their children—in a "manner worthy of full respect" and not abusive or altogether absent. Who in your world has modeled parenting well? What does that look like? Whether you are a parent, married without children, or single, how might those characteristics transfer to your circle of influence?

10. In another letter, Paul offers fathers brief instructions on how to raise their children. Read Ephesians 6:4. How do you think parents today can hold the tension between "not exasperat[ing]" their kids while simultaneously bringing them up "in the training and instruction of the Lord"? If you are a parent, is this challenging for you? How so? If you do not have children, in what areas can you influence children and youth?

11. Reread 1 Timothy 3:5. How does a leader's ability to "manage" their home or circle of influence transfer to a church or another organization?

12. In verse 6, Paul warns against moving a recent convert into an influential leadership position. Why do you think Paul insists that Christians develop spiritual maturity before assuming a leadership role?

13. Have you ever been given a responsibility that you weren't ready for? What happened? What did you learn?

DIGGING DEEPER

King David made a mess of his household by taking Bathsheba—another man's wife. In the shame-filled aftermath of his sin, he wrote, "Restore to me the joy of your salvation" (Psalm 51:12). Study the entire psalm. Why is it critical that leaders are emotionally and spiritually healthy before taking on a significant leadership position?

Most new believers experience deep joy upon receiving Jesus as their Savior, and this joy is sometimes accompanied by a zeal to jump right into ministry—sometimes into leadership positions. Paul advises leaders to be cautious of placing new believers in influential positions of leadership but instead to nurture that desire to lead while walking new Christ-followers through the process of discipleship.

14. Next, Paul cautions that those who become leaders before they are spiritually ready could "fall under the same judgment as the devil." Read Ezekiel 28:11–19 where the prophet Ezekiel describes the judgment that fell upon Satan. What flaw sparked his downfall (v. 17)? Why is this trap especially dangerous for leaders?

15. Paul's warnings apply to all of us. In what areas of life do you excel? Where has pride caused you to stumble? What can you do to keep yourself from becoming puffed up or conceited?

 Read 1 Timothy 3:8–13.

# INSTRUCTIONS FOR DEACONS

Now Paul turns to the qualifications for deacons (*diakonos*). Linda Belleville notes that the verbal form of *diakonos* "originally meant to wait on tables."[2] Later, the term was used in a broader sense to describe one who served. Today, the title of deacon could include an appointed, paid position, although many deacons are volunteers.

16. The qualifications for overseers and deacons are similar except the overseer must be "able to teach" (v. 2). Nevertheless, deacons "must keep hold of the deep truths of the faith with a clear conscience" (v. 9). Generally, what are "deep truths of the faith"? What do these two leadership characteristics tell you about what's required for church, ministry, and family health, or various other types of leadership?

17. Paul's exhortation to "keep hold of the deep truths of the faith" applies to us as well. What practices have you set in place to prioritize your relationship with Jesus? Where can you improve? What is one practice you could implement today?

18. Why do you think deacons should "first be tested" (v. 10) before being allowed to serve in the church? How should churches implement the testing process? What kind of people do you want to see in leadership positions in your church?

I (Rebecca) worked as a morning radio host for twenty years before taking a position at Dallas Theological Seminary. The year I stepped down, my boss brought in a consultant to assist the on-air staff in storytelling. I remember feeling frustrated and offended that I, a more-than-twenty-year veteran, had to sit through Radio 101 all over again. Later that day, I felt the Lord's conviction as I remembered what a mentor of mine once told me: "Always remain teachable." I realized my pride was keeping me from growing as a storyteller.

**DIGGING DEEPER**

Verse 9 in the NIV reads, "They must keep hold of the deep truths of the faith with a clear conscience." The Greek word for "deep truths" is *mustērion*, where we get our English word *mystery*. Paul used *mustērion* six times in his letter to the Ephesians: 1:9; 3:3, 4, 6, 9; and 6:19. Read these verses and explain what you think Paul meant when he said deacons "must keep hold of the deep truths [*mustērion*] of the faith." Why is this an important requirement for a deacon?

## Can Women Serve as Deacons?

First Timothy 3:11 presents a challenge to Bible interpreters. Verse 11 says:

> In the same way, the women [or wives] are to be worthy of respect, not malicious talkers but temperate and trustworthy in everything.

In Greek, the word *gunē* can mean either woman or wife. Some scholars believe Paul refers here to the wives of deacons while others believe he was laying out qualifications for female deacons. Thomas Schreiner argues that if Paul meant "wives" he would have added the word "their," to mean their (the deacons') wives, but because "their" is absent, he believes a more honest rendition of "woman" is in view.[4] This perspective opens the door to the possibility that Paul approved of women deacons.

Thomas Constable comes to the same conclusion but for different reasons:

> First, there is nothing about the office as such that would exclude a woman. Second, it would be unusual for Paul to prescribe qualifications for wives of deacons but not for wives of elders. Third, the fact that he inserted special qualifications for women in the middle of his list of deacon qualifications seems to indicate that he considered these women to be deacons (i.e., deaconesses).[5]

It does seem strange that Paul would only mention qualifications for deacons' wives but leave out qualifications for elders' wives. If he had been consistent the passage would look like this:

| | |
|---|---|
| Verses 1–7 | Qualifications for Male Elders |
| | Qualifications for Elders' Wives (Missing) |
| Verses 8–10 | Qualifications for Male Deacons |
| Verse 11 | Qualifications for Deacons' Wives |
| Verse 12 | An Additional Qualification for Male Deacons |

Thus, conservative theologians Schreiner and Constable agree that Paul may well have been listing the qualifications for female deacons in the early church, affirming historical records.

A look at early church history may provide direction and clarity. In AD 112, we find a reference to "women deacons" in a letter from Roman author and lawyer Pliny the Younger to the Emperor Trojan. Pliny compiled his huge collection of private letters into books before he died. These letters provide us with intimate details concerning public and private life during that time in the Roman Empire. In one of his letters, Pliny revealed that while investigating Christians, he tortured two Christian women whom he identified as "ministrae," or deaconesses in Latin.[6] Mike Aquilina elaborates:

The third century "Didascalia Apostolorum" ("Teaching of the Apostles") refers to deaconesses and tells bishops they should honor these women "as the Holy Spirit is honored." A later chapter describes the activities of deaconesses. . . . They can freely visit the homes of women who are sick, without causing scandal. They also played a major role in the baptism of women. In antiquity, Christians were baptized naked, many as adult converts. Since the clergy were male, deaconesses safeguarded the modesty of women, taking them into the water and completing the anointing that had been ceremonially begun by the bishop.[7]

Another review of records demonstrates that ecumenical councils, including the First and Second Council of Nicaea, the Ecumenical Council of Chalcedon, and the Council of Trullo, "endorsed the ordained diaconate of women for over six centuries."[8] Further, numerous Greek inscriptions through the sixth century reveal that women were assigned the title "deacon."[9]

Wherever you land on the issue of female deacons, we are first called to unity as fellow believers and then to influence others humbly and graciously in our various spheres of life.

19. What are two beautiful blessings Paul mentions when we serve well (v. 13)? Who benefits? Why are both so important in our lives?

20. Who are some contemporary women you would describe as honorable or worthy of respect? What do you admire about them?

Maintaining an "excellent standing" in the community was of major concern for the Ephesians because they lived in an honor/shame culture. Consider the cancel culture of the twenty-first century. One false move, one wayward tweet, and one's life can come crashing down. In much the same way, honor served as the currency of the first-century world. N. T. Wright and Michael Bird state, "For males, honour was acquired by showing courage, abilities, and trustworthiness."[10] Women were honored for showing hospitality to the stranger and charity to those in need. Shame, on the other hand, was avoided at all costs.

21. How do you feel after you've spent time serving—perhaps a day volunteering or a week on a mission trip? What does serving do for your heart? Did giving your time to others impact your relationship with Jesus? If so, how? How might "serving well" offer "great assurance in [your] faith in Christ Jesus"?

## CATHERINE OF SIENA—A TRUE SERVANT

Catherine was born in Siena, Italy, in 1347 in the middle of the Black Death—a plague estimated to have killed between thirty and sixty percent of the European population. Glahn writes, "Her parents' twenty-fourth child, Catherine lost a twin at birth, and a younger sister after her died as well, making her the youngest of a large family indeed."[11]

Known for extravagant generosity (which included giving away half her clothing and her family's food), Catherine devoted herself to Jesus at an early age. According to tradition, Jesus appeared to her in a vision when she was twenty-one and told her that she would minister to the sick.

Catherine was twenty-seven when the plague returned in 1374. Anyone who had the means to leave the crowded cities did, but not Catherine. While most people rushed out, Catherine and her followers rushed in to care for those who were sick and to bury those who had died.

# Belonging to a Peace-Loving Community

The tallest building in the world, the Burj Khalifa, towers over Dubai in the United Arab Emirates. Its 163 floors reach 2,717 feet into the sky, and a desert flower, the spider lily, inspired its design. Over 12,000 workers mixed more than ten million cubic feet of concrete to construct this mammoth skyscraper. For a building this tall to stand requires an incredibly strong foundation! Its base is thirteen feet thick and weighs more than 110,000 tons, the weight of approximately 100,000 elephants.

What the Burj Khalifa is to buildings, Christianity is to historical movements. Jonathan Hill writes,

> Today Christianity is the largest religion in the world, and is followed by approximately a third of the planet's population. It has spread beyond its ancient heartlands in Europe and the Middle East to North and South America, Asia, central Africa, and the Pacific. It is, by any standard, a significant element of modern culture. But it has played a major role in history too. Without Christianity, today's world would be very different in many ways.[1]

The church has played the most significant role in the influence of Christianity now and throughout the ages. The Lord doesn't expect you to do life solo; instead, he yearns for you to plug into and flourish in a healthy Christian community. And that community needs you!

Near the end of his earthly ministry, Jesus revealed to Peter, probably pointing to himself, "On this rock I will build my church, and the gates of Hades will not overcome it" (Matthew 16:18). Later Paul described the universal church as Jesus's body (Colossians 1:24). Since the first century, groups of Christians have gathered in local fellowships or "households of faith" to represent Christ to a chaotic, confused, and weary world.

I (Sue) love how our senior pastor greets the congregation on Sunday morning as "church," for that is what we are. The church is not a place; it's people, although they typically meet in some specified location, such as a home, a building, under a bridge, or wherever. Belonging to a group

---

**OPTIONAL**

Memorize 1 Corinthians 12:12–14

Just as a body, though one, has many parts, but all its many parts form one body, so it is with Christ. For we were all baptized by one Spirit so as to form one body— whether Jews or Gentiles, slave or free—and we were all given the one Spirit to drink. Even so the body is not made up of one part but of many.

of believers isn't optional for Christians. God expects us to nurture and strengthen one another so we can shine like stars in a dark world together (Philippians 2:15).

Sadly, however, from time to time my seminary students express dissatisfaction with their local churches. Sometimes their expectations are unrealistic. After all, the church is led by imperfect people still in process, but other times, their concerns are valid. Like many churches today, Ephesus was experiencing confusion and turmoil. Paul grieved over what he heard about them, and he sent Timothy, a young and trusted colleague, to help.

Paul's priceless advice to Timothy can also guide us as we do our part to support and encourage our local church to shine brighter and woo the world to Jesus. What would Jesus ask us to do to build a healthy local church body?

Paul begins with the priority of a sturdy foundation.

 Read 1 Timothy 3:14–16.

## REST IN THE LIFE-GIVING FOUNDATION

1. Have you ever belonged to a flourishing community of any kind (no names, please)? If so, when, and what difference did this experience make in your life? In your opinion, how vital to abundant living is being a part of a healthy community that nourishes its participants?

2. In verse 15 Paul identifies the ideal community. What is that community, and what words does Paul use to describe it? How is the church the "pillar and foundation" of the truth?

In Christ's person and work lies keys to the strength and flourishing of the faith community.[2]
—Robert Yarbrough

"The pillar and support of the truth" drew upon very familiar imagery in Ephesus. The imposing Temple of Artemis featured 127 pillars soaring 60 feet overhead to support a roof sixty percent larger than a regulation football field (425 feet by 225 feet). According to Paul, the Lord established the local church to become the support structure of divine truth.[3]
—Charles Swindoll

3. When a church is healthy, what good can it accomplish? If it's sick, what harm can it do? What has been your personal experience (no names, please)?

4. Also in verse 15, Paul reveals one reason he is writing this letter to Timothy. From what you have studied so far, how were some of the people in the church conducting themselves that resulted in chaos and confusion? Why did they need correction?

> Many of my close friends who've left the church have suffered real disappointment and hurt at the hands of Christians. Some have suffered tragic spiritual abuse by ministry leaders. It's no surprise, then, that they've moved away from Christian community. I mourn and grieve for anyone who has searched for God and family, only to find judgment, condemnation, and abuse. Lord, help us.[4]
> —Jeremy Linneman

5. God desires that all who belong to his "household" achieve "true godliness" through the help of the church. What is "true godliness" (v. 16)? What part do you think a healthy church plays in this process?

6. In verse 16 Paul referred to "the mystery from which true godliness springs." From Colossians 1:26, what did Paul mean by the term "mystery"? What is the rich truth revealed in Colossians 1:27? What do you think this means?

The hymn [3:16] describes what Christ did on earth in his humbled state and how his actions were received on earth and in heaven. There also may be a chronology that runs throughout the hymn and distinct parallelisms. Because the hymnic structure is so pronounced, it is almost universally recognized as a fragment of a hymn.[5]

—William Mounce

7. Paul describes more about this "mystery from which true godliness springs" in 1 Timothy 3:16. Who is it? What do you learn?

8. Why do you think Paul emphasized that Jesus must be the solid foundation of a healthy, life-giving church? What happens when something or someone else replaces that foundation?

For personal thought: Is your church community solidly resting on the foundation of knowing Jesus and his Word intimately? If your church rests on some other foundation, how likely do you think it is that you and others will grow strong in the Lord? Seek the Lord and possibly others concerning this important question.

 Read 1 Timothy 4:1–10.

## CONFRONT APOSTASY BIBLICALLY

Before we consider the issue of apostasy biblically, we need to define it. *Apostasy*, from the Greek verb *aphistēmi*, means to fall away from, to revolt, and to instigate others to do so. Apostates are people who deliberately choose to betray clear, sound doctrine and adopt rival systems of thought.

Swindoll writes,

One cannot accidentally become an apostate. Neither can one become guilty of apostasy over nonessential doctrines or issues that the Scriptures do not definitely address. For example, I disagree with theologians who do not accept immersion as the proper mode of baptism, but they are not apostate. A teacher becomes an "apostate" when he or she advances ideas that contradict the clear teaching of Scripture. Teaching is false when it undermines biblical truth, enables the teacher's sinful behavior, leads believers into sin, or preys upon the goodwill of listeners.[6]

9. Paul writes that apostasy will be common in "later times," a time-frame between Christ's first and second coming known as the church age. Where does apostasy originate (v. 1; Ephesians 6:12)? How might this reality influence how you confront apostates?

10. What examples of apostasy have you observed in churches today that distort sound doctrine and draw Christians away from pure biblical beliefs and practices? (No names, please, and be sure these examples are not personal preferences or disputable matters but involve contradicting the clear teaching of Scripture. If you are not sure, solicit insight from others.)

### DIGGING DEEPER

In Paul's letter to the Philippian church, he describes the different responses by others to his imprisonment (Philippians 1:12–18). What are they? What are the motives of those who are jealous of his ministry and now delight that Paul can no longer be as active for Christ as he had been in the past? How does Paul feel about them? Does he consider them apostates? What do you learn about apostates from this situation?

11. How does Paul describe apostates in 1 Timothy 4:2? What are some factors you think can cause someone to become an apostate?

Ephesus was a melting pot of ideas. If you visited a house church in Ephesus, you might meet a former Artemis worshipper, a converted Jew, and someone who had abandoned any one of a plethora of bizarre pagan philosophies circulating around the Roman Empire. This blend of differences easily leads to syncretism—combining various religious precepts into one faith practice. In addition, syncretism often challenged Timothy and other leaders as they attempted to teach and protect the pure doctrine that Paul brought when he founded the Ephesian church some ten years earlier.

12. From verse 3, what did one group of apostates teach? What two examples did Paul list? How did Paul refute this group's beliefs (vv. 3–4)?

13. From these two examples, what can you discern about the main thrust of their theology? Why do you think apostates often resort to these kinds of tactics?

14. Compare the following verses. What do these verses reveal about the falsity of these kinds of apostate teaching?

Genesis 2:23–24 and 1 Corinthians 7:8

Genesis 1:29 and 9:2–3

15. What does Paul suggest if you observe someone you think might be an apostate? What qualifies you to do this? What does Paul call you if you do this? (See 1 Timothy 4:6.)

16. Paul says to "point these things out to the brothers and sisters" (v. 6). What does pointing something out entail? What is the implied tone? What do you think Paul might be implying by calling these people "brothers and sisters"?

17. What do the following passages teach us about how to prepare our heart attitudes before we point out error? What precautions do we need to take?

Matthew 7:3–5

1 Peter 3:15–16

DIGGING DEEPER

John advised his friend Gaius concerning how to deal with apostates (3 John 9–10). He also warned other Christians about how to identify them (1 John 2:18–26). Jude, in his letter, addressed what believers need to know when apostates attempt to distort and pollute pure doctrine (Jude 3–16). Obviously, this danger is nothing new. Write an essay or create a chart synthesizing all you learn from these important passages on how to protect yourself and others from apostasy.

Some scholars translate *adelphoi* as "brothers" or "brethren," but the Greek word may also be used for "brothers and sisters" or "fellow Christians" depending on the context, and there is considerable nonbiblical evidence where the plural means "brothers and sisters."[7]
—NET Bible

# THE PROBLEM OF FORMER ARTEMIS WORSHIPPERS' HERETICAL TEACHING

Twice Paul refers to the danger of "myths" that pollute sound doctrine:

> As I urged you when I went into Macedonia, stay there in Ephesus so that you may command certain people not to teach false doctrines any longer or to devote themselves to myths and endless genealogies. Such things promote controversial speculations rather than advancing God's work—which is by faith. . . . (1 Timothy 1:3–4)

> Have nothing to do with godless myths and old wives' tales. (4:7)

As relatively new Christians, some female Ephesian converts were likely still under the influence of their past beliefs as Artemis worshippers, and some may have participated as leaders in that pagan priesthood. Out of ignorance and in desperate need of training in sound doctrine, they were spreading their false ideas. Thus, Paul rebuked those who "want to be teachers of the law, but they do not know what they are talking about or what they so confidently affirm" (1 Timothy 1:7). In 1 Timothy 4:7 Paul wrote, "But reject those myths fit only for the godless and gullible, and train yourself for godliness" (NET). The accompanying note by NET Bible scholars reads, "Those myths refer to the legendary tales characteristic of the false teachers in Ephesus and Crete."[8]

For more information about the mythological creation story of Artemis and her twin brother, Apollos, see page 42.

18. In verse 7, Paul identifies another group of apostates. On what did they base their false teaching? Without naming names, what modern-day examples can you identify that often counterfeit as people's ideologies and "religions"?

19. What does Paul suggest so we can identify and protect ourselves from these kinds of flawed "faiths" (vv. 7–10)?

20. In verses 8–10 Paul writes that physical fitness is "of some value," but he insists that "godliness" training is superior. Why? What does "godliness" training entail? In your opinion, what are women addicted to physical fitness hoping to accomplish? If you have dealt with related personal issues, share with your group why and what you've learned.

21. Why does Paul say we "labor and strive" (v. 10)? Would you say this is also your highest priority? Would others who know you well agree? Why or why not?

❋ Read 1 Timothy 4:11–16.

## RELENTLESSLY PURSUE "GODLINESS" TRAINING

Paul lists various priorities that Timothy is to "command and teach" here and throughout the letter (v. 11). Paul's admonitions to his dear son in the faith can benefit us all.

The currency of confusing and contradictory doctrine calls for ongoing instruction in the apostolic traditions (theology and ethics) to ensure conformity with the will of God as understood by the apostle [Paul].[9]
—Philip Towner

22. Timothy was probably younger than many people in the Ephesian churches. How does verse 12 apply to you? What can you learn if you are "younger"? What can you learn if you are "older"?

23. Obviously, the Holy Spirit had gifted Timothy in preaching and teaching (v. 13). Whatever your spiritual gift or gift-mix, how does verse 14 apply to you?

24. Finally, Paul instructs Timothy and us on our actions and attitudes as we strive to grow strong in our faith and live to please our blessed Savior. What are his instructions in verses 15 and 16? From the text, what are the two results we can expect?

25. How does it benefit others when they "see your progress" (v. 15)?

26. In this chapter of 1 Timothy, Paul reveals God's deep desire that his churches provide bastions of sound doctrine, healthy relationships,

and opportunities for his people to grow and serve together for their joy and his glory. Have you earnestly searched for a Christian community like this? If not, what has hindered you? If so, how can you build up your church and make it even better?

## THE DANCE OF THE PORCUPINES

Two porcupines dwelt at opposite ends of the forest, secluded, in the cold, lonely dark. Each longed to find warmth and light, authentic relationship, companionship, and a place to be fully known and loved. And so they journeyed to the middle of the forest and came together where they danced in their newfound friendship. But in time, because they were porcupines, they wounded each other, and bleeding, they each retreated back into the dark. But soon they missed their newfound friend and realized their wounds would only heal in the light, and so they leaped back into the dance, only to be wounded again.

Jeremy Linneman writes,

> Much of my pastoral ministry involves caring for and rehabilitating those who have suffered church hurt. I've discovered that *we're hurt in relationship, and we find healing in relationship*. . . . When we're sinned against by others, the natural tendency is to move away from everyone else. When we sin and are shamed by others, it's similarly natural to withdraw into ourselves. But while this withdrawal may be a natural survival instinct, it won't lead to complete healing. At some point, we must move toward others to find comfort and healing.[11]

# Contributing to a Peace-Loving Community

S ay "Girl Scouts" and most people think cookies, but my mind goes back to first grade and how much I (Rebecca) loved Wednesdays.

"On my honor, I will try
To serve God and my country,
To help people at all times,
And to live by the Girl Scout Law."

Along with the nine other girls in my troop, I recited the Daisy Promise at the start of every Girl Scout meeting. I remember it well: each Wednesday afternoon between 3:30 and 5:00 p.m., we'd meet for a lesson, a game, a snack, and a craft.

Mrs. Nesheim, our troop leader, would remind us that when we wore our sash or our vest, we represented something bigger than ourselves. "You belong to the Girl Scouts of America," she would say, "and that is an honor and a privilege."

An honor and a privilege, indeed, and one that carried expectations. The Girl Scout Law insists its members act with honesty and integrity. They are to respect authority, self, and others, to be kind and considerate. When everyone operates within the code of conduct, everyone wins.

What is true for the Girl Scouts is true for the church. Luke wrote of the earliest Christians,

All the believers were together and had everything in common. They sold property and possessions to give to anyone who had need. Every day they continued to meet together in the temple courts. They broke bread in their homes and ate together with glad and sincere hearts, praising God and enjoying the favor of all the people. And the Lord added to their number daily those who were being saved. (Acts 2:44–47)

The earliest church flourished because the earliest believers loved one another sacrificially and sought the good of the church over the good of

OPTIONAL

Memorize Philippians 2:3–4

Do nothing out of selfish ambition or vain conceit. Rather, in humility value others above yourselves, not looking to your own interests but each of you to the interests of the others.

self. In our next lesson, Paul encourages Timothy to exhort the believers in Ephesus to do the same.

## ✳ Read 1 Timothy 5:1–2.

## ENGAGING WITH YOUR SPIRITUAL FAMILY

The honor/shame culture of much of the ancient world turned nearly everything into a contest. David deSilva writes,

> People outside of an individual's kinship group, or outside an individual's extended household (which would include friends and clients or patrons), were viewed as potential rivals and sometimes even antagonists. Honor and its various components (wealth, fame, positions of influence, acknowledged precedence) were the prizes for which people competed with one another.[1]

1. In contrast, how did Paul want the believers in Ephesus to view one another?

    Older men as _____

    Older women as _____

    Younger men as _____

    Younger women as _____

    From verses 1 and 2, what picture did Paul have in mind when we interact with others in the church? How do you feel about this reality?

> The best way to be formed in Christ is to sit among the elders, listen to their stories, break bread with them, and drink from the same cup, observing how these earlier generations of saints ran the race, fought the fight, and survived in grace.[2]
> —James Frazier

2. How would you characterize your family of origin? Generally healthy? So broken that reconciliation isn't likely? Somewhere in between? How have your relationships with your family of origin affected your relationships in your church?

3. Read Matthew 12:46–50. How does Jesus define his family? What does that mean for those who grew up as only children wishing for siblings? Or who come from abuse or neglect? Or who never marry or have children? Or who have lost family members to tragic accidents?

4. Does your faith community feel like a family? Do you belong to any multigenerational groups? If you do, what are those relationships like? Why are multigenerational relationships important?

5. The NIV says we are to "exhort" older men as though they were fathers and older women as mothers (1 Timothy 5:1–2). The word *exhort* could also be translated "to correct," "to appeal to," or "to encourage." Have you ever felt you needed to correct an older person in your church or a parent or grandparent? What did you do? How did it go?

6. Paul told Timothy to treat younger men as brothers and younger women as sisters. Think back over the relationships in your life. What distinguishes your familial relationships from your friendships?

An ancient rabbi named Joshua ben Sirach wrote, "My child, help your father in his old age, and do not grieve him as long as he lives; even if his mind fails, be patient with him; because you have all your faculties, do not despise him. For kindness to a father will not be forgotten . . . in the day of your distress, it will be remembered in your favor . . . like frost in fair weather. Whoever forsakes a father is like a blasphemer, and whoever angers a mother is cursed by the Lord" (Ben Sirach 3:12–16 NRSV).

I (Rebecca) grew up as the oldest of three girls in our family of five. My sisters and I fought like cats and dogs when we were little, as do my two teenagers. In the ancient world, sibling rivalry would have brought a family deep shame. According to deSilva, "The relationship between siblings is the closest, strongest and most intimate of relationships in the ancient world. . . . We are accustomed to speak of sibling rivalry as a natural phenomenon but should be aware that such rivalry was a great evil in the classical world and to be guarded against completely or defused as soon as possible."[3]

**DIGGING DEEPER**

How did Jesus treat women "with absolute purity" in Luke 7:36–50 and John 8:2–11? What principles can you glean and model as you interact with the opposite sex?

God insisted that the Jews treat the most vulnerable members of society with honor. Moses warned the Israelites that God's wrath would burn against all who mistreated widows or orphans (Exodus 22:22–24), and the psalmist painted God as the one who "sustains the fatherless and the widow" (Psalm 146:9). In the New Testament, Jesus went out of his way to show compassion to a grieving widow when he raised her only son from the dead (Luke 7:11–17).

7. If you've missed out on close sibling relationships in your family of origin, have you experienced those in your faith family? If so, how did you create those relationships? If not, how might you cultivate them in the future?

8. Paul instructs men to treat women "with absolute purity" (v. 2). Note that this specific instruction is given to *men*, the gender with more power in the ancient world. But women are not exempt. How can men and women treat each other with "absolute purity"?

## INSTRUCTIONS ON CARING FOR WIDOWS

In the ancient world, a woman's livelihood depended mainly on the men in her life—first her father, then her husband, and if her husband died, her sons. Were a woman to lose her husband before bearing children, she was left in a dire situation.

> When her husband died, she could return to her own family if the purchase price was paid back to the husband's heirs or the dowry to the wife's family. Otherwise, she had to remain in the husband's family, where she took an even more subordinate and often humiliating position. In many cases, she was not allowed to remarry. This is why many widows preferred death at the burial of their husbands to further life without them.[4]

 Read 1 Timothy 5:3–8.

9. How does our society today esteem widows? In your opinion, how well does the Christian church care for them? How might the church ascribe value or worth to widows in your congregation?

10. Do you know a widow who falls into the category of being "really in need"? Put yourself in her shoes for a moment. What do you think would minister to her the most?

Paul differentiates between "widows who are really in need" and widows who have children and grandchildren. In the ancient world, government offered no social security, Medicare, or assisted living establishments. The family was God's answer to caring for aging parents.

11. How did Paul advise the widow who was "really in need" because she was without family or they refused to care for her (v. 5)?

12. The Jewish leaders had orchestrated elaborate ways for grown children to shirk their responsibilities toward their elderly parents. Read Mark 7:8–13 and explain what they were doing that caused Jesus to firmly rebuke them. Why do some grown children abandon their elderly parents today?

The phrase "give proper recognition" in 1 Timothy 5:3 comes from the Greek word *timaō*, which can also be translated as ascribing value or worth to someone.

We truly are seeing the aging of a nation. As a result, churches of all sizes are facing the needs of maturing adults. The challenge has reached both rural and inner city congregations among all ethnic groups. . . . The conclusion? Pastors, church leaders, and lay people must be equipped to meet the needs of mature adults in the twenty-first century.[5]
—David Gallagher

There I sat, a follower of Christ, somehow trying to balance the reality of all the pain Alzheimer's disease would inflict on us with the hope of God's care and eternal life in heaven. Without thinking I responded, "I guess I'm going to live on the other side of eternity." I would do my best to focus on the eternal, to trust the One who held eternity in His hands, the One who had gone ahead to prepare a place for us and would come back to take us to be with Him (John 14:3).[6]

—Cynthia Fantasia, upon learning of a loved one's diagnosis

13. Next, in 1 Timothy 5:4, Paul instructs widows' children and grand-children. What are they to do and why? What does this suggest that God wants for us concerning our own families?

14. Do you believe there's ever a time when an elderly parent forfeits their children's or grandchildren's care? For abusive or absent parents, when would healthy boundaries be wise? How might undeserved honor or compassion affect an unrepentant parent?

15. Remember that in the ancient world no government assistance existed for the elderly, and the family was God's answer to caring for aging parents. Today's world operates differently. Can you think of an occasion where honoring one's father and mother might look more like finding compassionate care for them?

16. In verses 5 and 6, Paul makes another distinction—this time between the widow who "is really in need" and the "widow who lives for pleasure." What do you think Paul means when he says the latter woman is "dead even while she lives"? See Ephesians 4:18 for a clue.

In verse 6, the Greek word translated "pleasure" is *spatalaō* and paints a picture of plump sheep living in lush pastures[7]—in other words, those who indulge themselves in the lap of luxury.

17. Paul calls a Christian who fails to provide for family "worse than an unbeliever" (1 Timothy 5:8). What does it say to the watching world if a Christian refuses to care for a parent or grandparent?

 Read 1 Timothy 5:9–16.

## ENROLLING WIDOWS FOR ASSISTANCE

Who were the widows that ancient churches put on some kind of list for assistance? Scholars continue to wrestle with this question. The Greek word translated as "widow" in the New Testament had some elasticity. *Chēra* meant a married woman who had lost her husband, but it could also mean a woman who had never married. Ignatius of Antioch, an early church father from the second century, wrote, "I salute the households of my brethren with their wives and children, and the virgins who are called widows."[8]

Theologian John Stott (and others) propose that "widow" may also have been an office of the early church, similar to the office of deacon.[9] Polycarp, a disciple of the apostle John, in his letter to the Philippian church, said, "Our widows must be sober-minded as touching the faith of the Lord, making intercession without ceasing for all men, abstaining from all calumny, evil speaking, false witness, love of money, and every evil thing, knowing that they are God's altar."[10] Paul may have been talking about enrolling widows into this order or office in 1 Timothy 5:9–10.

18. Today widows face different obstacles, but in some respects, single mothers could be considered twenty-first-century "widows." How might God want Christians to care for them?

19. Paul insinuates that for a widow to be enrolled for church assistance (placed on the list), she must meet both physical and spiritual qualifications (vv. 9–10). List them in the space below. Why do you think Paul required these qualifications (v. 16)?

In the United States in 2021, the average age a woman married for the first time was almost twenty-nine years old.[11] With more career and education opportunities today than in any other period in history, many women wait to tie the knot until they've settled into a career. In the first century, parents commonly arranged marriages for their daughters as young as thirteen.

20. What was one reason Paul advised Timothy not to put "younger widows" on the list (vv. 11–12)? What kind of impression might that behavior make on watching unbelievers?

21. In verse 13 Paul raised another concern related to "younger widows." What is it? Have you observed some young women displaying this behavior? How might this verse be applied to women and social media? Gossiping? Engaging in unhealthy pastimes? If you are "young," what insight can you bring to the discussion? If you are "older," what have you learned through experience?

22. Have you or someone you know found yourselves in a situation where you were "idle," with few meaningful activities or work to fill the time? What are the dangers? What are some helpful antidotes?

23. In this part of the letter, Paul has communicated advice for the compassionate administration of a church's resources to serve women in need. In light of these principles, how do you think Paul would counsel the church today to minister to single women and working mothers?

24. What can the church do to help women in need feel seen and heard today?

25. As you draw out principles you've gleaned from Paul, what is the Holy Spirit saying to you?

How might you personally live out these same principles in light of the tremendous needs of women today?

Natalie Reid-Knutson lost her husband, Wayne, to a sudden heart attack in August of 2018. Instantly, she found herself a widow trying to raise three young boys on her own.

As their first Christmas without Wayne drew near, Natalie booked four plane tickets to New York City. She couldn't bear the thought of the holidays in their home without her husband.

The hustle and bustle of the Big Apple helped ease the pain of their grief. They stayed with a family-friend-turned-tour-guide, who knew all the fun activities and places to see. In New York, Natalie realized she and her sons needed to move forward with their lives and create new memories. When she returned home to Texas, God placed a vision on her heart to help young widows and their kids navigate the first few years of life without a parent or spouse.

Now, Natalie and her second husband, Kjell, own and operate Broken Halos Haven, a grief getaway in the heart of Oldtown Lewisville and fifteen minutes from the Dallas/Fort Worth airport. Widows and their children stay for free and choose from a list of specially curated activities to create a gift registry that friends and family can purchase from. The three-day, two-night escape is designed to minister deeply to grieving hearts and is Natalie and Kjell's way of loving widows with the love of Christ.

# Harmony Help for Leaders, Workers, and Supervisors

LESSON 7

If you've parented a wayward child, Monica knows your pain. Of her three children, she shed the most tears for her oldest son. Monica married young, and her husband disapproved of her faith. When their son, Augustine, fell ill, she begged her husband to allow her to baptize the young boy, but he refused.[1]

Her husband was known for his fiery temper and philandering ways, and Monica was devastated when Augustine appeared to follow in his father's footsteps. Her devastation, however, proved no match for her devotion. Monica insisted that her son read the Scriptures as part of his education. She prayed day and night for his soul. During one particularly rebellious season, she made Augustine leave their family home. Monica brought her concerns to a church leader, who advised her that her son was not yet ready to commit his life to the Lord. Monica doubled down, spending hours at a time in prayer.

Later in life, St. Augustine, Bishop of Hippo, reflected on his mother's life and the pain he caused her. He wrote:

> Receive my confessions and thanksgivings, O my God, for innumerable things which I am silent in. But omit I will not whatsoever my soul can bring forth concerning that handmaid of thine, which brought forth me: both in her flesh, that I might be born to this temporal light, and in her heart too, that I might be born again to the eternal light.[2]

Today, Christians worldwide remember Augustine as one of the most prominent leaders of the developing church. Augustine, however, would probably beckon us to turn our admiration first to the Lord and then to his mother, who ultimately led their entire family to Christ.

**Read 1 Timothy 5:17–18.**

OPTIONAL

**Memorize Ezekiel 34:2–5**

**This is what the Sovereign Lord says, "Woe to you shepherds of Israel who only take care of yourselves! . . . You have not strengthened the weak or healed the sick or bound up the injured. You have not brought back the strays or searched for the lost . . . So they were scattered because there was no shepherd, and when they were scattered they became food for all the wild animals."**

After discussing how churches and families should care for widows in the church, Paul moves on to provision for another group.

1. First, Paul says that faithful servant leaders in the church should receive "double honor" (v. 17). What do you think this means? Read the following verses and summarize them in your own words.

   Galatians 6:6

   1 Corinthians 9:13–14

   Luke 10:5–7

2. Assess your expectations of leaders. Are you realistic, remembering that leaders are finite and still in process? At the same time, leaders are held to a higher standard (James 3:1). What do you think is the balance between giving grace to leaders when they make mistakes while keeping them accountable for leading well and with integrity?

Not many of you should become teachers, my fellow believers, because you know that we who teach will be judged more strictly.
—James 3:1

3. What two tasks does Paul mention (1 Timothy 5:17)? Why do you think he draws attention to these two tasks?

4. According to Ephesians 4:11–13, what is a primary task of church leaders? Have you observed leaders who do this well? If so, describe how. In contrast, some leaders disregard these important instructions. Without mentioning names, what did they do and how did this failure affect the health of the ministry?

5. Think back to a time you received recognition or affirmation for a contribution you'd made. What was the situation? How did it make you feel?

6. Who are some of the faithful leaders God has placed around you? What do you admire about them? How have they made a difference in your life?

**DIGGING DEEPER**

Study 1 Corinthians 12 and answer these questions: Does God esteem some spiritual gifts and abilities over others? Value Christian vocational leaders more than lay leaders or people who serve behind the scenes? Regard Christians who minister in the church over Christians who minister in the secular world? Why or why not?

**DIGGING DEEPER**

Read Deuteronomy 25:4 and 1 Corinthians 9:1–13. What do you think is the purpose of Old Testament law regarding the ox?

7. Some church leaders are paid staff and others are volunteers. Some of them write curricula, teach, organize, evangelize, and lay counsel, pouring time, effort, and affection into the people they nurture. Specifically, what are some ways they could be given "double honor" when they are not paid staff members? When they are?

 Read 1 Timothy 5:19–25.

## PAUL'S CHARGE TO CORRECT SINFUL LEADERS PUBLICLY

In 1996, three couples started a home Bible study. By 2013, the study group had grown into a well-known megachurch. Mars Hill Church spanned fifteen locations, welcomed thousands of guests each Sunday, and distributed online content to hundreds of thousands of viewers. By 2015, the church had disbanded. The reason? Corruption from the top down.

In addition, in recent years multiple churches, ministries, and schools have been accused of covering up leaders' sexual abuse and in the process damaging their credibility and Jesus's reputation. This travesty must also have been occurring in the early church, considering Paul's stern admonition to correct and not show favoritism toward leaders who abuse their power.

Paul's next words emphasize the importance of integrity in leadership.

8. In verse 19 Paul provides a guideline to help churches, ministries, and schools deal with anyone bringing accusations against leaders. What is it? Why do you think this guideline is necessary?

*Christianity Today* released a podcast called *The Rise and Fall of Mars Hill*, detailing the events preceding and following the church's demise. To find out more, visit https://www.christianity today.com/ct/podcasts /rise-and-fall-of-mars-hill.

### DIGGING DEEPER

Paul's first letter to the Corinthian church contained serious rebukes for the way that church dealt with sexual sin in their midst. Digest chapter 5 and write out principles that would help ministries today handle leader and member abuse biblically.

9. Have you ever been falsely accused? What happened? How did you feel? What about a leader you know (no names, please)? What damage can result?

The word translated "who are sinning" is a present active participle, which gives the term a continuous force. Essentially, this means Paul is referring to a leader who continues to sin, even after a private confrontation.

10. Paul left instructions concerning those leaders "who are sinning" in verse 20. However, the apostle John says in 1 John 1:8–10 that we all sin from time to time. What kinds of "sins" do you think Paul might be talking about? See 1 Peter 5:2–3 for an example.

11. When a leader is definitely caught "sinning," what does Paul charge the church, ministry, or school to do? What does Paul hope to see as a result of public correction? (1 Timothy 5:20)

12. Why is public reproof of leaders "who are sinning" vital to the reputation of the ministry and the protection of congregants? Why is it difficult but necessary?

Often spiritual abusers use Scripture out of context. . . . Preventing spiritual abuse is difficult because tangible evidence remains elusive. But one effective way to combat spiritual abuse is to encourage biblical literacy. When believers know the Word of God for themselves, they are better able to detect false teaching, including false teaching that seeks to influence behavior or to misuse authority.[3]
—Misty Hedrick

Paul protects leaders from frivolous accusations and makes sure they are protected by ensuring that a number of people, usually other leaders, are involved to thoroughly investigate the claim. However, if the claim is found to be true, Paul demands protection for any who have been hurt or damaged by the leader's serious sin. As difficult and heartbreaking as this action might be, if leaders' serious sins are covered up, they are free to continue in this sin, harming others, and other leaders will be encouraged to do the same. Time after time, this reality has proven to be true, has ruined well-meaning leaders concerned about the sinful leader's reputation, and has muddied the name of Jesus and his body. Paul demanded tough love for the long-term good of all. —Sue

13. What are some reasons churches, ministries, or schools might disregard Paul's charge in verse 20?

First Timothy 5:21 represents what secular scholars call an "oath formula"—invoking the names of gods to "strengthen certain commands and instructions and to put the stamp of divine authority on them."[5] We see biblical authors, including Paul, use the oath formula in various places (for example, 2 Corinthians 11:11 and Galatians 1:20). However, this particular formula—calling on these three divine witnesses—only occurs here in all of Scripture, in the context of leaders continuing in sin. We cannot overstate the significance of Paul's words.

14. Who are the three witnesses looking on to ensure that Christians obey this "charge" (1 Timothy 5:21)? What does this reveal about the seriousness of Paul's admonition?

15. Different churches, ministries, and Christian schools have chosen to obey or ignore Paul's charge in varied ways. Have you ever seen this admonition obeyed well? Poorly? If so, describe what happened (no names, please).

16. What is at stake if Paul's charge is not carried out? If the leader's sin is covered up? What examples can you provide that have resulted in damage to people as well as ultimately to the ministry?

17. Paul concludes his charge in verses 21–22 with a serious warning about not showing favoritism. Why might a church, ministry, or school be tempted to show favoritism or partiality when one of their own is caught sinning?

18. After studying Paul's command and considering this issue, how do you feel about his instructions to acknowledge a leader's sinning in some public way?

19. Churches appointed leaders by praying and laying their hands on them. What is Paul's warning in verse 22? In light of Paul's previous charge in verses 20–21, why should the church move slowly when selecting leaders?

20. Verse 22—moving slowly when appointing leaders—sets the context for verses 24 and 25. Both good deeds and hidden sins can take time to uncover. What should you do if someone new to a ministry wants to teach or lead in some way that they may not be qualified to do?

Authors Scot McKnight and Laura Barringer point out that fear-based church cultures begin when "powerful pastors become associated too easily with God in the minds of the congregation" and people seek the pastor's approval, which they equate with God's approval.[7] In power- and fear-based cultures, the authors point out, secrecy reigns with only insiders knowing about decisions and judgments. And those "in the know" use power and fear to control and silence people.[8]

The biblical authors issue stern warnings on wagging tongues and sharing secrets (Romans 1:29; 2 Corinthians 12:20) and herald those who maintain confidentiality (Proverbs 11:13; 25:9). But where do we draw the line? Over the past few years, investigators have uncovered multiple stories of church abuse, and often the victims were silenced with Scripture taken out of context. If someone in a leadership position violates someone in any way, the right thing to do is to report it immediately. —Rebecca

Someone traumatized is not thinking linearly— they need support, not advice. . . . Sexual abuse is traumatic. If you haven't walked through it yourself, don't assume you know how soul crushing it is.[9]
—Mary DeMuth

"God does not show favoritism" (Romans 2:11; Galatians 2:6). "But if you show favoritism, you sin" (James 2:9).

Playing favorites doesn't end in adolescence. Even the wisest among us needs a reminder that the church is no place for partiality.

21. You've heard it said, "You can't judge a book by its cover." In other words, it takes time to get to know a person's heart. Have you ever found yourself in a situation where someone was not who they appeared to be? Without using names, what happened? What did you learn from the situation?

### ❁ Read 1 Timothy 6:1–2.

Next, Paul addresses another difficult situation likely plaguing the Ephesian church. Slaves who had found freedom in Christ were chafing under the yoke of slavery and showing disrespect to their masters.

Whenever ancient social practices like slavery or polygamy occur in the Bible, we can easily question why God didn't address the issue then and there. Clearly, the Bible teaches that God abhors injustice and expects us to as well. It's helpful to understand that throughout the Bible, God plants seeds that culminate in the Christian social norms of a one-man, one-woman marriage and the abolition of slavery. For example,

> The Old Testament begins a long, redemptive process which ultimately overturns the institution of slavery. It begins with establishing a Sabbath day rest for slaves (Ex. 23:12), release of slaves in the seventh year (Lev. 25:39–43), provision for slaves upon release (Deut. 15:12–18) and capital punishment for slave traders (Deut. 24:7). This redemptive movement culminates in the New Testament where Paul pleads with Philemon to release Onesimus from slavery and relate to him on the basis of Christian brotherhood. While some claim the household codes in Paul's epistles affirm slavery, the reality is that these household codes actually served to protect slaves from human cruelty. The clear trajectory of Scripture is moving away from the practices of slavery and toward freedom.[12]

As Christianity affects people's morality, these injustices should be brought to light and no longer tolerated. And praise God, we can look forward to eternal life where justice will roll down like a river (Amos 5:24).

In the meantime, we can apply general principles taught in these verses to our workplace situations. Granted, there is a difference. As employees, we are free to leave our jobs, and abuse in the workplace should never be excused.

However, since many Christians spend the majority of their time there, finding ways to honor Christ in the workplace is important. And, it's often there that we can show nonbelievers the beauty of a relationship with Jesus.

22. What do the following verses teach about the worker/supervisor relationship?

    1 Timothy 6:1

    Ephesians 6:5–8

    1 Peter 2:18–23

23. If you are a supervisor, how should you treat those who work for you (Ephesians 6:9)?

24. What attitudes in our culture today make the admonitions in this lesson difficult for some to follow? Regardless of what a society teaches is "right and wrong," why do biblical principles and mandates take precedence?

**DIGGING DEEPER**

Read Romans 12:9–21. How should Paul's instructions direct our approach to the biblical principles taught in this lesson? Why do you think this matters?

25. How might Christian organizations as well as people's lives be far better if society's norms were ignored and biblical principles and mandates were followed carefully? How might this affect your own life?

## A Tale of Four Churches

In her 2019 memoir *What Is a Girl Worth?* Rachael Denhollander describes her story of sexual abuse within the microcosm of USA gymnastics. Team doctor Larry Nassar had abused her for years (continuing through attempted cover-ups by coaches and USAG authorities) under cover of providing medical treatment. Her public accusation led to hundreds of other gymnasts coming forward with similar accusations. As late as summer 2021, more gymnasts were testifying, some before the US Congress, of Nassar's abuse.

Sadly, Denhollander relates her experience against the backdrop of four local churches. Preferring to keep issues like sexual abuse concealed, two churches avoided the issue that consumed her life at the time.[13] But two others opened their doors and arms to comfort, encourage, and support the Denhollanders as they fought for justice for more than a hundred abuse survivors throughout a tumultuous case.

In her book, Denhollander writes candidly about her struggle to maintain faith in a church culture so focused on the victimizer that the victim often goes unacknowledged. In fact, in the case of the latter, church leaders often focus only on the injured party's need to avoid bitterness and prematurely forgive rather than heal brokenness and seek justice.[14]

*—Misty Hedrick[15]*

# Steps to Contentment in Your Community

Christian contentment is the gracious inward work of God in your life. We usually think of contentment as a personal blessing, but the Bible also speaks about the joy of being content in your faith community. Are you content there? Until you are, you'll miss one of life's most precious treasures. Dietrich Bonhoeffer described what can easily occur if we hold unrealistic expectations of our faith communities.

> She who loves her dream of a community more than the Christian community itself becomes a destroyer of the latter, even though her personal intentions may be ever so honest and earnest and sacrificial. . . . She enters the community of Christians with her demands, sets up her own law, and judges the brothers and sisters and God Himself accordingly. . . . Because God has already laid the only foundation of our fellowship, because God has bound us together in one body with other Christians in Jesus Christ, long before we entered into common life with them, we enter into that common life not as demanders but as thankful recipients.[1] [Gender pronouns changed]

As Paul begins to wrap up his letter, he shows us how contentment is the Holy Spirit's glorious gift of well-being in our faith communities. We come together to worship in peace and encourage one another in spiritual growth.

Jump in as Paul shares the secrets of contented community life without angst, competition, and bickering. Isn't there enough chaos outside the church? Blessed are the peacemakers.

## ❋ Read 1 Timothy 6:3–9.

Paul returns to the primary reason he wrote this letter to Timothy—to combat the chaos resulting from apostates infiltrating the church with messages that contradicted the pure teaching of Jesus Christ and the verbal

**OPTIONAL**

**Memorize Philippians 4:11–13**
I have learned to be content whatever the circumstances. I know what it is to be in need, and I know what it is to have plenty. I have learned the secret of being content in any and every situation, whether well fed or hungry, whether living in plenty or in want. I can do all this through him who gives me strength.

and written messages of the apostles. As you may recall from lesson 5, an apostate is someone who renounces or abandons their former religious principles and often attempts to influence others to do the same. In addition, Timothy needed to confront naive believers who were influenced by these apostates and were spreading their propaganda (v. 3).

Paul begins by pointing out three negative qualities of these troublemakers. Understanding these qualities helps us be on the alert for intentional or unintentional apostates today who can easily disrupt church communities' corporate peace.

1. God wants to bless you with personal and communal contentment. On a scale of 1 to 10, how would you rate yourself in these vital areas of life?

**Personal contentment**

1 (discontent)_____10 (richly content)

**Faith community contentment**

1 (discontent)_____10 (richly content)

## PORTRAIT OF AN APOSTATE

2. What is the first characteristic of an apostate (v. 4; see also 3:6)? Define this word.

3. How would someone who has developed this quality act? Without naming names, describe a person you've known who exhibited this attribute. How do you think a person becomes this way?

4. How can you fight against ever developing this trait yourself?

5. We've just observed Paul exposing conceited people who are creating chaos in the church in Ephesus. In 2 Timothy 3:1–7, he warns Timothy again. What additional insight can you glean about these renegades from this second letter?

6. Why do you think Paul exhibits such strong emotions when describing these false teachers and those repeating their messages? If you have experienced the damage people like this can do in a church, describe the fallout (no names, please).

In 1 Timothy 6:4, Paul adds a second description of these troublemakers. He says they are deluded and bereft of understanding. By placing "nothing" first in this Greek clause, Paul may be implying "understands absolutely nothing," a hyperbolic but telling charge.[6]
—Robert Yarbrough

7. Apostasy can be found on social media today, from uninformed "influencers" to casual comments by naive or angry contributors. How can you ensure that you uphold your Christian integrity if you engage in social media? How can you ensure that you are not duped?

My goal is that they may be encouraged in heart and united in love, so that they may have the full riches of complete understanding, in order that they may know the mystery of God, namely, Christ, in whom are hidden all the treasures of wisdom and knowledge. I tell you this so that no one may deceive you by fine-sounding arguments.
—Colossians 2:2–4

Where is the chaos of false teaching that leads to discontentment most likely to erupt in the twenty-first century? Social media. Facebook, Instagram, Twitter . . . of course none of these platforms existed in Paul's day, but the principles we're learning from 1 Timothy are timeless truths that affect how and why we post and what we like and share.

8. Paul paints a third attribute of these apostates in 1 Timothy 6:4 by writing that these argumentative people have an unhealthy _____ in _____ and _____ about _____.

From your study so far, what kinds of controversies do you think led people in the Ephesian church to develop these unhealthy tendencies? What kinds of words easily cause dissension in our church bodies today?

9. What do you think is the difference between a healthy interest and an unhealthy interest in controversial topics? How might the first lead to peace while the second lead to disunity?

10. How do the following passages prepare you to be a peacemaker as you interact with your Christian brothers and sisters?

Matthew 5:14–16

1 Peter 3:15

Colossians 4:4–6

11. If you tend to have an "unhealthy interest in controversies and quarrels about words" (1 Timothy 6:4), what problems has this tendency brought about in your relationships with family, friends, and in your church? How might you overcome these tendencies?

**DIGGING DEEPER**

Read Philippians 1:27 and Ephesians 2:11–22. What does Paul remind them about their citizenship, and what does he call them to do together?

Contentment is a state of the heart; not a state of affairs.[9]
—Linda Dillow

## THE CONSEQUENCES OF APOSTATES' NEGATIVE BEHAVIOR

12. Paul goes on to describe what results from unhealthy bickering over divisive issues in the church (vv. 4–5). They are listed below:

envy

strife

malicious talk

evil suspicions

constant friction

What happens when a church community is characterized by these kinds of actions and attitudes?

Usually, the sort of people who find themselves in constant quarrels would be in such quarrels no matter what religion, or no religion, they inhabit. . . . Quarrels are mostly about the very same thing: not about persuading opponents or making a difference in the world but causing the quarreler to feel alive.[10]
—Russell Moore

13. Paul writes that churches who tolerate these attitudes and actions allow naive Christians to be "robbed of the truth" (v. 5). Who robs them? What happens to people who are "robbed of the truth"? How can you ensure you are never "robbed of the truth"?

Various groups in the early church had a common denominator that is still a massive temptation today, namely, to focus on some secret or special knowledge available only to a select group in the church, which sets them above the rest of the "common herd." . . . But such secret so-called knowledge is not only false knowledge of God, it is destructive to the unity of the faith and the bond of love that must typify the Christian community.[11]
—Jeffrey Weima and Steven Baugh

Imagine how awful it would feel to have your child say to you, "I don't really love you or want your love, but I *would* like my allowance, please." Conversely, what a beautiful gift it is to have the one you love look you in the eye and say, "I love you. Not your beauty, your money, your family, or your car. Just *you*." Can you say that to God?[12]
—Francis Chan

You are rich if you have enough to meet your most basic needs. You are rich if you have access to clean water, food, shelter, love, a roof over your head (that doesn't leak), people who love you, a job. . . . You have to count your blessings to see that you are richer than you think.[13]
—Michelle Singletary

### DIGGING DEEPER

Analyze Acts 5:1–11. How did Ananias and Sapphira's sin impact their relationships with their faith community?

Thou awakest us to delight in Thy praise; for Thou madest us for Thyself, and our heart is restless, until it repose in Thee.[14]
—Saint Augustine

14. What often motivated these rabble-rousers in the Ephesian church (v. 5)? Why might people fall into an identical trap today? How can faith communities guard against this danger?

15. In contrast to verse 5, what does Paul say is really "great gain" (v. 6)? What two qualities must be partnered for Christians to experience this "great gain" both in their personal lives and in their sacred communities?

16. Why do people who do not follow the Lord or live according to his direction find genuine contentment elusive?

17. What will you take with you from this earth when you die physically (v. 7)? How should this sobering reality affect how you live now?

18. Jesus taught beautiful truths using analogies and word pictures to show how loving money destroys contentment. What imagery did he use, and what do you learn in the following passages?

| | Imagery | Lesson |
|---|---|---|
| Matthew 6:19 | earthly treasures eaten by moths and rats, stolen by thieves | money easily disappears |
| Matthew 6:24 | | |
| Matthew 6:25–27 | | |
| Matthew 6:28–34 | | |

19. What general principle do you think Paul was teaching in 1 Timothy 6:8? Do you agree with this idea? What do you believe would enable you to be content in your personal life and in a faith community?

20. What typically happens to people who make money the top priority in their lives (vv. 9–10)? How can they easily damage themselves, their loved ones, and their faith community? Can you share examples (no names, please)?

DIGGING DEEPER

Jesus told whole parables and stories to help us understand the foolishness of valuing money and what it can buy. Dissect, retrieve principles, and write out what you discover from the parable of the rich fool (Luke 12:13–21).

At the time Paul wrote to Timothy, the staple foods in Ephesus were bread dipped in wine or olive oil, fish, and vegetables and fruit in season. Occasionally, after a public sacrifice, they might enjoy oxen or a fowl. Otherwise, meat and fish was usually salted or stored in a jar of honey because refrigeration did not exist.[15]
—Jeffrey Weima and Steven Baugh

You'll never see a U-Haul behind a hearse.[16]
—Denzel Washington

Money may not buy love, but fighting about it will bankrupt your relationship.[17]
—Michelle Singletary

21. According to Paul, money and the possessions it buys aren't evil in and of themselves. What makes them evil (v. 10)?

**DIGGING DEEPER**

Study Acts 2:42–47; Philippians 1:27; and John 13:34–35. What do you learn about how God desires a healthy Christian community to function and why?

22. What kinds of material possessions lure you to love them? How might you resist the temptation to take these desires to dangerous levels that can pollute your contentment?

Contentment is the equilibrium between the enjoyment of life now and the anticipation of what is to come.[18]
—Priscilla Shirer

23. What can you learn from Proverbs 30:7–9 to help ensure you never endanger your contentment by loving money?

24. Glance back at question 1. From what you learned in this lesson, how can you up your contentment factor in both these arenas?

## REQUIRED FOR CONTENTMENT

My (Sue's) church was a healthy church with people of all ages, rich Bible teaching, and opportunities to serve and grow inside and outside the church. Soon we joined a small "home group" where we met regularly with a diverse community of believers and where our faith skyrocketed. Of course, no church is perfect, but overall, the leaders exhibited strong servant leadership and genuine humility. The church community thrived, and we were content there for about ten years.

Then sadly, through a series of poor decisions, infighting among the leadership resulted in a heart-wrenching church split. Some of our friends walked away from the Lord; others left to join other congregations. Unsure what to do, we stayed, but the church never fully recovered, and ultimately for the good of our children, God led us out too.

Today, we love our church. It's not perfect either, since it's full of sinners, including us, but we don't take the blessing of a generally life-giving faith community for granted, especially after witnessing the devastating demise of our first church.

In Paul's letter to Timothy, he assumes that involvement in a church will be the norm for every Christian. You won't experience authentic spiritual growth or contentment in life without it. Find a healthy church. Invest to keep it that way. It's more valuable than anything you can buy, and in a real sense—unlike almost anything else—you can take it with you.

# Flee the Enemy's Traps and Take Hold of the Life

As a child, I (Sue) dreamed of becoming a piano virtuoso, my adept fingers racing up and down the keys to light up sounds of symphonic beauty. I envisioned myself gliding across the stage, full-length gown glittering, then seating myself at a grand piano and attacking the instrument with such fervor that my enraptured audience leapt from their seats to express their astonishment.

In third grade, I persuaded my parents to pay for piano lessons, and I eagerly awaited the first one. What a disappointment! First, my teacher insisted I memorize a silly poem, "Every Good Boy Does Fine," or some such nonsense, as I recall. And my songbook reeked of diddly tunes like "Row, Row, Row Your Boat" and "Mary Had a Little Lamb." By the time the recital rolled around, I still hadn't graduated to Beethoven or Rachmaninoff—truth be told, I hadn't even mastered *Songbook One*. Why? Because instead of practicing the expected hour a day, I chose to go outside and play with friends, and sadly, my dream of becoming a piano virtuoso never materialized.

My friend Sarah shared a similar dream, and when I would knock on her door to ask her to come out and play, she respected that sixty-minute timer and declined until it dinged. Her practice times increased over the years, and in college she chose to study under the tutelage of a master musician. She realized her dream of becoming a piano virtuoso.

As Paul concludes his letter to Timothy, he instructs his protégé to "take hold of the life that is truly life" (6:19). As an adult, I attended one of Sarah's performances, and as I watched in awe, Sarah stepped onto the stage, gown glittering, sat down, and "took hold" of that piano. Alas, despite all my good intentions and pitiful efforts, I will never "take hold" of a piano. However, we, as believers, can all apply that same diligence to "take hold" of eternal life.

Taking hold of the life that is truly life means that our efforts to please God go straight to the top of our priority list. Paul's final words to Timothy are jam-packed with insight for us as well as action verbs—flee, pursue, fight, take hold, charge, command, lay up, turn away, and guard.

OPTIONAL

Memorize 1 Timothy 6:12

Fight the good fight of the faith. Take hold of the eternal life to which you were called when you made your good confession in the presence of many witnesses.

Sick and tired of drowning in chaos? Paul shows us how to "take hold of the life that is truly life," but not without action on your part. Are you ready to truly take hold?

## ❀ Read 1 Timothy 6:11–16.

> The separation from all that is evil (as exemplified in the case of the heretics in 6:3–10) is underscored with two direction-changing devices: "but you" and the following traditional "flee/pursue" formula. . . . In this sense, the subtext of Paul's instruction—flee/pursue—is "become what you are in Christ." . . . That is to say, in a very real sense the present experience of Christian life is a continual process of flight from and pursuit toward.[1]

1. In verse 11 Paul addresses Timothy as, "But you, man of God." However, his instructions are appropriate for every believer. Insert your name in the phrase below and read it aloud.

   But you, _____, woman of God, flee from all this and pursue righteousness, godliness, faith, love, endurance, and gentleness.

   Which of the six qualities do you most need to take hold of right now? Why?

2. In verse 12 Paul compares the believer's life to a fight or a war: "Fight the good fight of the faith." However, we do not fight like non-believers. From the passages below, what can you learn to enable you to valiantly fight for your faith?

   Philippians 3:12–14

   2 Corinthians 10:3–5

Ephesians 6:12

1 Timothy 1:18–20

Paul instructs us to fight the good fight with passion, boldness, and tenacity. How did Jacob illustrate these qualities when he wrestled with God in Genesis 32:22–32?

3. The Greek word translated "fight" is *agonizomai*. What English word does this Greek word sound like? What do you think Paul is attempting to reveal to us when he uses this Greek word to describe our attempts to live a faithful life?

The way I see it, if you want the rainbow, you gotta put up with the rain![3]
—Dolly Parton

## LOOKING BACK (1 TIMOTHY 6:12; 2 TIMOTHY 4:7)

4. What else does Paul ask Timothy to remember in 1 Timothy 6:12? When did you make "your good confession in the presence of many witnesses"? What are varied ways we show we are Christians? How does remembering this help us to "fight the good fight of the faith"?

5. In Paul's second letter to Timothy, Paul revealed that he believed his remaining time on earth was short. As he looked back to assess his life, how did Paul sum it up in 2 Timothy 4:7? As you look back and assess your days on earth so far, what words would you use to summarize them?

The unexamined life is not worth living.
—Socrates, at his trial for corrupting youth, where he was subsequently sentenced to death

## LOOKING FORWARD (1 TIMOTHY 6:13–15; 2 TIMOTHY 4:8)

6. What did Paul look forward to when his days on earth concluded (2 Timothy 4:8)? Why did he believe he would receive the "crown of righteousness," and who else, according to this passage, is a candidate? Who would place this crown on his head? When?

**DIGGING DEEPER**

Study the crowns mentioned in the Bible in the note at the end of this lesson on pages 110–11. Which do you believe you might receive and why?

Only one life, 'twill soon be past,
Only what's done for Christ will last.[4]

—C. T. Studd

7. What do the passages below tell us about rewards that faithful Christians can expect? Will all Christians receive the same rewards? Support your answer from Scripture.

Matthew 16:27

Ephesians 6:7–8

Jeremiah 17:10

1 Corinthians 3:5–9

8. Read 1 Corinthians 3:10–15 carefully.

What is the foundation on which all believers must build (v. 11)?

What do you think is the difference between building on that foundation using "gold, silver, [and] costly stones" instead of "wood, hay or straw"? How do you discern the difference?

Remembering that God values service up front and behind the scenes equally, in your opinion, what might be some good examples of both categories?

How will each builder's works be tested to see whether they are works of "gold, silver, [and] costly stones" or works of "wood, hay or straw" (vv. 12–13)?

If a builder's works survive the test, what will result (v. 14)?

If a builder's works do not survive the test, what will result (v. 15)?

What do you believe Paul is attempting to explain to Christians in this passage?

He is no fool who gives what he cannot keep to gain what he cannot lose.[5]
—Jim Elliot, martyred Christian missionary

9. Where must all Christians appear to receive their rewards that are due them "for the things done while in the body" (2 Corinthians 5:6–10)? How do you know that these verses refer only to believers?

See the notes at the end of this lesson on pages 109-10 for more insight into the "judgment seat of Christ," also known as the *bēma* seat.

10. Read Revelation 20:11–15. From what you can discern between the "judgment seat of Christ" in 2 Corinthians 5:10 and the "great white throne judgment" in the Revelation passage, how are these two judgments different?

11. Reread 1 Timothy 6:13–15. What is Paul's charge to Timothy and to us all?

What command do you think Paul is talking about?

Why do you think Paul encourages Timothy, and us, to look ahead to the glorious future appearing of our Lord Jesus Christ and his rewards? How does this perspective help us as we attempt to flee the traps of the devil that ensnared the apostates and pursue "the life that is truly life"?

12. When have you experienced a time when you needed to stand up for your faith? What have you learned from Paul's advice to Timothy that can help during times of trials and testing?

13. In 6:15, Paul concludes this section of his first letter by bursting into glorious praise to God in the form of a hymn or doxology. As we know, the first-century Ephesians lived in a culture that encouraged them to worship many gods and goddesses, including the Roman emporer and Artemis. How might this doxology counter worship of these false gods? What false gods does your culture encourage you to worship?

 Read 1 Timothy 6:17–21.

Child, you have to learn to see things in the right proportions. Learn to see great things great and small things small. When you stand at the gate of eternity, as I did in the concentration camp, you see things from a different perspective than when you think you may live for a long time. Every time I saw smoke pouring from the chimneys of the crematorium, I asked myself, "When will it be my turn to be killed or to die?" And when you live like that every day, in the shadow of the crematorium, there are very few things that are really important—or only one—to share with as many people who will listen about the Lord Jesus Christ who is willing that anyone who wants to can come to Him.[6]
—Corrie ten Boom, Dutch survivor of the Holocaust

For our struggle is not against flesh and blood, but against the rulers, against the authorities, against the powers of this dark world and against the spiritual forces of evil in the heavenly realms.
—Ephesians 6:12

Immortal, invisible, God only wise, in light inaccessible hid from our eyes, most blessed, most glorious, the Ancient of Days, almighty, victorious, thy great name we praise.[7]
—Walter Smith

14. Wrapping up, Paul returns to his earlier theme that greed is a powerful distraction that we must fiercely battle if we are to win the fight that results in eternal rewards (vv. 17–18). Lay out the principles that Paul encourages Timothy to teach Christians, both then and now.

15. What are the benefits that Paul promises in v. 19? Are you "taking hold of the life that is truly life"? Why or why not?

Believers live in an eschatological tension. They live in this age and must address themselves to the needs around them. But they also belong to the eschatological kingdom and must conduct themselves with an eye to what will be. By working out their salvation in practical ways such as sharing, they are transferring their riches to the coming age. . . . The reason for doing so, apart from recognizing one's true position in the present age as a recipient of God's gracious gifts, is the desire to grab on to life that is truly life: eschatological life, eternal life.[8]
—William Mounce

16. Paul ends his first letter to Timothy the same way that he began, emphasizing his primary concern. Compare verses 20–21 with 1 Timothy 1:3–7. Why do we need to take foolish talk, godless chatter, and false doctrine so seriously? What is at stake?

17. What distortions, myths, and controversial speculations have you observed infiltrating the Christian church today, resulting in confusion and chaos? (Please don't mention specific people, churches, or denominations.) What have you learned in this study that might help you be part of the solution to return to the true gospel?

## DIGGING DEEPER

Jesus taught a parable to the crowd related to storing up treasure in our eternal futures. Analyze the parable in Luke 12:13–21. What do you think it means to be "rich toward God" (12:21)?

## Wise Perspective as an Antidote to Chaos

Perspective makes all the difference. Anyone who has cared for a newborn baby knows that those first few weeks are beautiful but chaotic, grueling, exhausting, hormonal, and painful. It's tempting to zoom in on the moment and feel lost in the cycle of feeding, burping, and diapering while trying to heal, get a bit of sleep, and not be overwhelmed by the chaos. If you are like me, whenever we're in a stressful season, we are tempted to lose perspective and zoom in, often resulting in a skewed outlook.

At the end of Paul's first letter to Timothy, he encourages Timothy to zoom out—to look back, to look forward, and to look up. Looking back reminds us of all the ways God has shown himself faithful so far. Looking forward reminds us of our destination in the heavenly kingdom and the rewards we will experience at the judgment seat of Christ. Looking up reminds us that Jesus loves us, always has our best interest at heart, and is worthy of our complete trust.

Have you lost yourself in the stress of this moment? Do the difficulties of your season, the anxiety of the daily news, or an overwhelming schedule cause you to lose focus? Take Paul's advice to Timothy seriously and zoom out. This moment is not forever. This is not the end. Create beauty out of the chaos. Cultivate an eternal perspective to help you endure and enjoy each moment in light of the beautiful story God is writing in your life.

—*Lisa Adams*

## Notes on the Judgment Seat of Christ (aka the Bēma Seat) and Crowns

### 1. The Judgment Seat of Christ (aka the Bēma Seat)

Jesus often told us to expect rewards for what we do on earth. For example, "But love your enemies, do good to them, and lend to them without expecting to get anything back. Then your reward will be great" (Luke 6:35).

In his letter to the Corinthians, Paul explains that when we die physically, our spirit separates from our body for a time while we wait for Jesus to resurrect our bodies during the rapture. He goes on to tell us about another important event in our eternal lives—the time we stand before Jesus to give an account of our earthly lives, receive rewards or not, and learn about what we will be and do when we reign with Christ and serve as priests in his millennial kingdom (Revelation 4:9–11). This moment, called the judgment seat of Christ, or the bēma seat, happens right after the rapture.

Therefore we are always confident and know that as long as we are at home in the body we are away from the Lord. For we live by faith, not by sight. We are confident, I say, and would prefer to be away from the body and at home with the Lord. So we make it our goal to please him, whether we are at home in the body or away from it. For we must all appear before the judgment seat of Christ, so that each of us may receive what is due us for the things done while in the body, whether good or bad. (2 Corinthians 5:6–10)

First, let's be clear. The judgment seat does not determine whether or not you are saved from the wrath of God. If you have accepted Jesus as your Savior, you will never experience the great white throne judgment, where nonbelievers will be judged. This judgment seat of Christ is not to punish sin, but believers are still accountable to God, as Paul states in 1 Corinthians 4:2–5.

Now it is required that those who have been given a trust must prove faithful. I care very little if I am judged by you or by any human court; indeed, I do not even judge myself. My conscience is clear, but that does not make me innocent. It is the Lord who judges me. Therefore judge nothing before the appointed time; wait until the Lord comes. He will bring to light what is hidden in darkness and will expose the motives of the heart. At that time each will receive their *praise* from God. (emphasis added)

The Greek word for "judgment seat," *bēma*, refers to a raised platform similar to where the judge sits in a courtroom or where rewards are distributed at athletic games. What's the purpose of the *bēma*? To assess the quality of our service. I must admit I (Sue) find this truth frightening. I know my motives aren't always pure, and I don't want to serve Jesus to gain notoriety or to feel good about myself, but sometimes I do. However, I hope this realization sobers my intentions and causes me to lay aside those ugly ulterior motives. And then I simply must rely on his mercy and grace. In some just way, Jesus will assess the value of what we've become and done and reward us accordingly. What kinds of service does he value? A look at different kinds of "crowns" may provide some insight.

## 2. Crowns

Jesus advised Christians to do good works to please God and not other people: "Be careful not to practice your righteousness in front of others to be seen by them. If you do, you will have no reward from your Father in heaven" (Matthew 6:1). The Bible also mentions specific honors, called "crowns," that will be given for specific practices:

The Crown of Rejoicing (1 Thessalonians 2:19)
  For believers who lead others to Christ

The Crown of Glory (1 Peter 5:1–4)
  For shepherding God's people graciously and faithfully

The Crown of Righteousness (2 Timothy 4:8)
  For believers who long for Jesus's return and live a righteous
  life in light of that reality

The Crown of Life (James 1:12; Revelation 2:10)
  For believers who endure suffering for their faith, even unto
  death

The Imperishable Crown (1 Corinthians 9:24–25)
  For believers who exhibit consistent self-discipline leading to
  victory

What will we do with these crowns? We will fall down at the feet of
Jesus and lay our crowns before him in humble recognition of the reality
that he enabled us to achieve these honors. These awards will also influence what we do in the coming millennial kingdom (Luke 19:11–26).

# About the Authors

**SUE EDWARDS** is professor of educational ministries and leadership (her specialization is women's studies) at Dallas Theological Seminary, where she has the opportunity to equip men and women for future ministry. She brings more than forty years of experience into the classroom as a Bible teacher, curriculum writer, and overseer of several megachurch women's ministries. As minister to women at two megachurches in Dallas, she has worked with women from all walks of life, ages, and stages. Her passion is to see modern and postmodern women connect, learn from one another, and bond around God's Word. Her Bible studies have ushered thousands of women all over the country and overseas into deeper Scripture study and community experiences.

With Kelley Mathews, Sue has coauthored *Organic Ministry to Women: A Guide to Transformational Ministry with Next Generation Women* and *Leading Women Who Wound: Strategies for an Effective Ministry.* Sue and Kelley joined with Henry Rogers to coauthor *Mixed Ministry: Working Together as Brothers and Sisters in an Oversexed Society. Organic Mentoring: A Mentor's Guide to Relationships with Next Generation Women,* coauthored with Barbara Neumann, explores the new values, preferences, and problems of the next generation and shows mentors how to avoid potential land mines and how to mentor successfully. She coedited with DTS Vice President for Education and Professor of Educational Ministries and Leadership, George M. Hillman Jr., to write *Invitation to Educational Ministry: Foundations of Transformative Christian Education.* This book serves as a primary academic textbook for schools all over the country as well as a handbook for church leaders. Sue teamed up again with Kelley to write their newest book *40 Questions About Women in Ministry,* released in 2022.

Sue earned a doctor of ministry degree from Gordon-Conwell Theological Seminary in Boston, a master's in Bible from Dallas Theological Seminary, and a bachelor's degree in journalism from Trinity University. With Dr. Joye Baker, she oversees the Dallas Theological Seminary Doctor of Educational Ministry degree with a women-in-ministry emphasis.

Sue has been married to David for fifty years. They have two married daughters, Heather and Rachel, and five grandchildren. David is a retired CAD applications engineer and a lay prison chaplain. Sue loves fine chocolates and exotic coffees, romping with her grandchildren, and taking walks with David and their two West Highland terriers, Quigley and Emma Jane.

**REBECCA CARRELL** is a Bible teacher, conference speaker, and author. After spending more than twenty years as a broadcaster on the radio in Dallas/Fort Worth, she now mentors and ministers to students at Dallas Theological Seminary in the Media Arts and Worship Department as she works toward her doctorate in educational ministry.

Rebecca hosts and produces the podcast *Honestly, Though: Real Talk. Real Life. Real Faith.* Her books include *Holy Jellybeans: Finding God through Everyday Things*, *Holy Hiking Boots: When God Makes the Ordinary Extraordinary*, and *Anxious for Nothing: An Inductive Study of Paul's Letter to the Philippians*.

She and her husband, Mike, are the proud parents of two teens—Caitlyn and Nick. Connect with Rebecca on Twitter, Instagram, Facebook, or through RebeccaCarrell.com.

# Notes

## How to Get the Most Out of a Discover Together Bible Study

1. Howard G. Hendricks and William D. Hendricks, *Living by the Book: The Art and Science of Reading the Bible* (Chicago: Moody, 2007), 23.

## Why Study 1 Timothy?

1. Clinton E. Arnold, *Power and Magic: The Concept of Power in Ephesians* (Eugene, OR: Wipf and Stock, 2001), ix.
2. Paul Trebilco, *The Early Christians in Ephesus from Paul to Ignatius* (Grand Rapids: Eerdmans, 2004), 13.
3. Trebilco, *Early Christians in Ephesus*, 14.
4. Trebilco, *Early Christians in Ephesus*, 17.
5. Sandra L. Glahn, "The Identity of Artemis in First Century Ephesus," *Bibliotheca Sacra* 172 (July–September 2015): 316–34.
6. B. M. Metzger, "St. Paul in Ephesus and the Magicians," *Princeton Seminary Bulletin* 38 (1944): 27.

## Lesson 1

1. CultureofChaos, "Culture of Chaos—An Introduction," *Medium*, August 29, 2020, https://thecultureofchaos.medium.com/culture -of-chaos-an-introduction-2f1ab90cce5c.
2. Clinton E. Arnold, *Power and Magic: The Concept of Power in Ephesians* (Eugene, OR: Wipf and Stock, 2001), 18.
3. Tara Isabella Burton, *Strange Rites* (New York: PublicAffairs, 2020), 120–21.
4. Harriet B. Braiker, *The Disease to Please: Curing the People-Pleasing Syndrome* (New York: McGraw-Hill, 2001), 33.
5. William D. Mounce, *Pastoral Epistles*, Word Biblical Commentary, vol. 46 (Nashville: Thomas Nelson, 2000), 30.
6. Robert W. Yarbrough, *The Letters to Timothy and Titus* (Grand Rapids: Eerdmans, 2018), 101.

7. Charles Ryrie, "The End of the Law," *Dr. Ryrie's Articles* (Bellingham, WA: Logos Bible Software), 89.

### Lesson 2

1. Philip H. Towner, *The Letters to Timothy and Titus*, New International Commentary on the New Testament (Grand Rapids: Eerdmans, 2006), 162.
2. Saint Ignatius of Loyola to Francisco de Borja, Duke of Gandía, September 20, 1548, Woodstock Theological Library Digital Collection, Georgetown University, https://library.georgetown.edu/woodstock/ignatius-letters/letter11.
3. Robert W. Yarbrough, *The Letters to Timothy and Titus* (Grand Rapids: Eerdmans, 2018), 164.
4. Yarbrough, *Letters to Timothy and Titus*, 164–65.
5. Find illustrations of first-century Greek and Roman women in Rolf Hurschmann, "Hairstyle," in *Brill's New Pauly Encyclopedia of the Ancient World*, ed. Hubert Cancik and Helmuth Schneider (Leiden: Brill, 2005), 5:1099; James Wiener, "Ancient Hairstyle of the Greco-Roman World," World History Et Cetera, December 9, 2015, https://etc.worldhistory.org/interviews/ancient-hairstyles-of-the-grecoroman-world; Dr. Katharine Schwab and Dr. Marice Rose, "Hair in the Classical World," Bellarmine Museum, Fairfield University, Fairfield, CT, October 16, 2015, https://www.youtube.com/watch?v=QpiaSjWQ5RM; and "Hairstyle and Headgear in Ancient Greece. Historical Greek Fashion," World4U, December 14, 2019, https://world4.eu/hairstyles.
6. Richard B. Hays, *First Corinthians*, Interpretation: A Bible Commentary for Teaching and Preaching (Louisville: John Knox, 2011), 185–86.
7. Sandra Glahn, "Who Were the Women with Shaved Heads (1 Cor. 11:5)?," *Engage*, September 30, 2014, https://blogs.bible.org/who-were-the-women-with-shaved-heads-1-cor-115.
8. Bruce W. Winter, *Roman Wives, Roman Widows: The Appearance of New Women and the Pauline Communities* (Grand Rapids: Eerdmans, 2003), 104.
9. Amy Carmichael, *Candles in the Dark: Letters of Hope and Encouragement* (Fort Washington, PA: CLC, 1982), 53.

### Lesson 3

1. Sue Edwards and Kelley Mathews, *40 Questions About Women in Ministry* (Grand Rapids: Kregel Academic, 2022), 307.
2. Johannes P. Louw and Eugene Albert Nida, *Greek-English Lexicon of the New Testament: Based on Semantic Domains* (New York: United Bible Societies, 1996), §37.21.

3. H. G. Liddell, *A Lexicon: Abridged from Liddell and Scott's Greek-English Lexicon* (Oak Harbor, WA: Logos Research Systems, 1996).

4. Timothy Friberg and Barbara Friberg, *Analytical Lexicon of the Greek New Testament* (Grand Rapids: Baker, 2000).

5. *Lexham Analytical Lexicon to the Greek New Testament* (Oak Harbor, WA: Logos Research Systems, 2008–2013).

6. Barclay M. Newman Jr., *A Concise Greek-English Dictionary of the New Testament* (Stuttgart: German Bible Society, 1993).

7. *Enhanced Strong's Lexicon* (Oak Harbor, WA: Logos Bible Software, 1995).

8. William Witt, *Icons of Christ: A Biblical and Systematic Theology for Women's Ordination* (Waco: Baylor University Press, 2020), 146.

9. John Knox, quoted in William J. Webb, *Slaves, Women & Homosexuals: Exploring the Hermeneutics of Cultural Analysis* (Downers Grove, IL: InterVarsity, 2001), 265.

10. Wayne Grudem, *Evangelical Feminism and Biblical Truth* (Sisters, OR: Multnomah, 2004), 68.

11. Michelle Lee-Barnewall, *Neither Complementarian nor Egalitarian* (Grand Rapids: Baker Academic, 2016), 144.

12. John Calvin and William Pringle, *Commentaries on the Epistles to Timothy, Titus, and Philemon* (Bellingham, WA: Logos Bible Software, 2010), iii.iv.iv.

13. Witt, *Icons of Christ*, 161.

14. Ben Witherington, *Women in the Earliest Churches*, Society for New Testament Studies Monograph Series, vol. 59 (New York: Cambridge University Press, 1988), 122.

15. Clinton E. Arnold, *Power and Magic: The Concept of Power in Ephesians* (Eugene, OR: Wipf and Stock, 2001), 21.

16. Mike Greenberg, "Who Was the Twin of Artemis?," Mythology Source, September 23, 2020, https://mythologysource.com/who-was-the-twin-of-artemis.

17. NET Bible, Second Beta Edition (Richardson, TX: Biblical Studies Foundation, 1996, 2003), 2180, note 9.

18. Sandra Glahn, "The First-Century Ephesian Artemis: Ramifications of Her Identity," *Bibliotheca Sacra* 172, no. 688 (October–December 2015): 463.

19. Andreas J. Köstenberger and Margaret E. Köstenberger, *God's Design for Man and Woman: A Biblical-Theological Survey* (Wheaton: Crossway, 2014), 211.

20. Thomas R. Schreiner, "Women in Ministry," in *Two Views on Women in Ministry*, 2nd ed., ed. James R. Beck and Craig L. Blomberg (Grand Rapids: Zondervan Academic, 2005), 108.

21. Douglas Moo, "What Does It Mean Not to Teach or Have Authority over Men? (1 Timothy 2:11–15)," in *Recovering Biblical Manhood*

and Womanhood: A Response to Evangelical Feminism, ed. John Piper and Wayne Grudem (Wheaton: Crossway, 1991), 192.

22. Andreas Köstenberger, "Saved Through Childbearing?," *CMBW News* 2, no. 4 (September 1997), https://cbmw.org/wp-content/uploads/2013/05/2-4.pdf.

23. Köstenberger and Köstenberger, *God's Design*, 216.

24. Philip B. Payne and Andrew Bartlett are among the heterarchs adopting this view. George Knight, as well as church fathers Tertullian, Ignatius, Irenaeus, are among hierarchs who do.

25. Donald Todman, "Childbirth in Ancient Rome: From Traditional Folklore to Obstetrics," *Australian and New Zealand Journal of Obstetrics and Gynaecology* 47, no. 2 (April 2007): 82–85, https://doi.org/10.1111/j.1479-828X.2007.00691.x.

26. Sandra L. Glahn, "The Identity of Artemis in First-Century Ephesus," *Bibliotheca Sacra* 172 (July–September 2015): 319.

27. Glahn, "Identity of Artemis in First-Century Ephesus," 319.

28. Gary G. Hoag, *Wealth in Ancient Ephesus and the First Letter to Timothy: Fresh Insights from* Ephesiaca *by Xenophon of Ephesus*, Bulletin for Biblical Research Supplements 11 (Winona Lake, IN: Eisenbrauns, 2015), 228.

### Lesson 4

1. William Arndt et al., *A Greek-English Lexicon of the New Testament and Other Early Christian Literature* (Chicago: University of Chicago Press, 2000), 870.

2. Linda Belleville, "Commentary on 1 Timothy," in *1 Timothy, 2 Timothy, Titus, and Hebrews*, Cornerstone Biblical Commentary 17 (Carol Stream, IL: Tyndale, 2009), 71.

3. Thomas D. Lea and Hayne P. Griffin Jr., *1, 2 Timothy, Titus*, The New American Commentary, vol. 34 (Nashville: B&H, 1992), 116.

4. Thomas Schreiner, "Does the Bible Support Female Deacons? Yes," The Gospel Coalition, February 19, 2019, https://www.thegospelcoalition.org/article/bible-support-female-deacons-yes.

5. Thomas L. Constable, "Notes on 1 Timothy," *Constable's Expository (Bible Study) Notes*, 2022 edition, 79, http://planobiblechapel.org/tcon/notes/pdf/1timothy.pdf.

6. Mike Aquilina, "Special Report: Can There Be Women Deacons?" Angelusnews.com, February 22, 2019, https://angelusnews.com/voices/special-report-can-there-be-women-deacons.

7. Aquilina, "Special Report: Can There Be Women Deacons?"

8. John Wijngaards, "Church Councils on Women Deacons," Wijngaards Institute for Catholic Research, http://www.womendeacons.org/history-church-councils-women-deacons. See also John Wijngaards, *The Ordained Women Deacons of the Church's First Mil-*

*lennium* (Norwish, UK: Hymns Ancient and Modern, 2012), 18–19.

9. Gary Macy, "The Ordination of Women in the Early Middle Ages," *Theological Studies* 16, no. 3 (2000): 481–507.

10. N. T. Wright and Michael F. Bird, *The New Testament in Its World: An Introduction to the History, Literature, and Theology of the First Christians* (Grand Rapids: Zondervan Academic, 2019), 114.

11. Sandra L. Glahn, "A Christian Response to Ebola," *Bible.org*, October 14, 2014, https://blogs.bible.org/a-christian-response-to-ebola.

## Lesson 5

1. Jonathan Hill, *What Has Christianity Ever Done for Us? How It Shaped the Modern World* (Downers Grove, IL: InterVarsity, 2005), 6.

2. Robert W. Yarbrough, *The Letters to Timothy and Titus* (Grand Rapids: Eerdmans, 2018), 220.

3. Charles R. Swindoll, *1 & 2 Timothy, Titus*, Swindoll's Living Insights New Testament Commentary, vol. 11 (Carol Stream, IL: Tyndale, 2014), 74.

4. Jeremy Linneman, "We're Hurt, and Healed, in Community," The Gospel Coalition, May 18, 2021, https://www.thegospelcoalition.org/article/hurt-healed-community.

5. William D. Mounce, *Pastoral Epistles*, Word Biblical Commentary, vol. 46 (Nashville: Thomas Nelson, 2000), 215.

6. Swindoll, *1 & 2 Timothy, Titus*, 81.

7. NET Bible, Second Beta Edition (Richardson, TX: Biblical Studies Foundation, 1996, 2003), 2180, note 7, translator's note.

8. NET Bible, 2180, n. 9.

9. Philip H. Towner, *The Letters to Timothy and Titus*, New International Commentary on the New Testament (Grand Rapids: Eerdmans, 2006), 321.

10. Thomas L. Constable, "Notes on 1 Timothy," *Constable's Expository (Bible Study) Notes*, 2022 edition, 96, http://planobiblechapel.org/tcon/notes/pdf/1timothy.pdf.

11. Linneman, "We're Hurt, and Healed, in Community," italics in original.

## Lesson 6

1. David deSilva, *Honor, Patronage, Kinship & Purity: Unlocking New Testament Culture* (Downers Grove, IL: IVP Academic, 2000), 166.

2. James Frazier, "All Generations of Saints at Worship," in *Across the Generations: Incorporating All Ages in Ministry: The Why and How*, ed. Vicky Goplin et al. (Minneapolis: Augsburg, 2001), 56.

3. DeSilva, *Honor, Patronage, Kinship & Purity*, 166–67.

4. Gustav Stählin, "Χήρα," in *Theological Dictionary of the New Testament*, ed. Gerhard Kittel, Geoffrey W. Bromiley, and Gerhard Friedrich (Grand Rapids: Eerdmans, 1973), 442.

5. David P. Gallagher, *Senior Adults Ministry in the 21st Century: Step-by-Step Strategies for Reaching People Over 50* (Eugene, OR: Wipf and Stock, 2006), 6–7.

6. Cynthia Fantasia, *In the Lingering Light: Courage and Hope for the Alzheimer's Caregiver* (Colorado Springs: NavPress, 2019), 4.

7. William Arndt et al., *A Greek-English Lexicon of the New Testament and Other Early Christian Literature* (Chicago: University of Chicago Press, 2000), 936.

8. Joseph Barber Lightfoot and J. R. Harmer, *The Apostolic Fathers* (London: Macmillan, 1891), 159.

9. John R. W. Stott, *Guard the Truth: The Message of 1 Timothy & Titus*, The Bible Speaks Today (Downers Grove, IL: InterVarsity, 1996), 132.

10. Lightfoot and Harmer, *The Apostolic Fathers*, 178.

11. United States Census Bureau, "Median Age at First Marriage: 1890 to Present," Census.gov, https://www.census.gov/content/dam/Census/library/visualizations/time-series/demo/families-and-households/ms-2.pdf.

### Lesson 7

1. Augustine of Hippo, *St. Augustine's Confessions*, 2 vols., ed. T. E. Page and W. H. D. Rouse, trans. William Watts, Loeb Classical Library (New York: Macmillan, 1912), 1:33.

2. Augustine, *St. Augustine's Confessions*, 2:35.

3. Misty Hedrick, "How Can We Make Churches and Other Ministries Safer for Women?" in Sue Edwards and Kelley Mathews, *40 Questions About Women in Ministry* (Grand Rapids: Kregel Academic, 2022), 319.

4. *New International Dictionary of New Testament Theology and Exegesis*, ed. Moisés Silva (Grand Rapids: Zondervan Academic, 2014), 239.

5. Daniel C. Arichea and Howard Hatton, *A Handbook on Paul's Letters to Timothy and to Titus*, UBS Handbook Series (New York: United Bible Societies, 1995), 130.

6. Mary DeMuth, "10 Ways to Spot Spiritual Abuse," MaryDeMuth.com, September 6, 2016, https://www.marydemuth.com/spiritual-abuse-10-ways-to-spot-it.

7. Scot McKnight and Laura Barringer, *A Church Called Tov: Forming a Goodness Culture That Resists Abuses of Power and Promotes Healing* (Carol Stream, IL: Tyndale, 2020), 35.

8. McKnight and Barringer, *A Church Called Tov*, 37–38.

9. Mary DeMuth, *We Too: How the Church Can Respond Redemptively to the Sexual Abuse Crisis* (Eugene, OR: Harvest House, 2019), 171–72.

10. Henry Cloud and John Townsend, *Safe People: How to Find Relationships That Are Good for You and Avoid Those That Aren't* (Grand Rapids: Zondervan, 1995), 62.

11. Hedrick, "How Can We Make Churches and Other Ministries Safer for Women?," 321.

12. Timothy Tennent, "Slaves, Women and Homosexuals," Seedbed, February 23, 2013, https://seedbed.com/slaves-women-and -homosexuals.

13. Rachael Denhollander, *What Is a Girl Worth? My Story of Breaking the Silence and Exposing the Truth about Larry Nassar and USA Gymnastics* (Carol Stream, IL: Tyndale Momentum, 2019), 220.

14. Denhollander, *What Is a Girl Worth?*, 99.

15. Originally published in Misty Hedrick, "How Can We Make Churches and Other Ministries Safer for Women?," in Sue Edwards and Kelley Mathews, *40 Questions About Women in Ministry* (Grand Rapids: Kregel Academic, 2022), 317. Printed with permission.

### Lesson 8

1. Dietrich Bonhoeffer, *Life Together: A Discussion of Christian Fellowship*, trans. John W. Doberstein (New York: Harper & Row, 1954), 27–28.

2. Julie A. Gorman, *Community That Is Christian: A Handbook for Small Groups*, 2nd ed. (Grand Rapids: Baker Books, 2002), 24.

3. Charles R. Swindoll, *1 & 2 Timothy, Titus*, Swindoll's Living Insights New Testament Commentary, vol 11 (Carol Stream, IL: Tyndale, 2014), 130.

4. Heather Zempel, *Community Is Messy: The Perils and Promise of Small Group Ministry* (Downers Grove, IL: InterVarsity, 2012), 45.

5. Bonhoeffer, *Life Together*, 112.

6. Robert W. Yarbrough, *The Letters to Timothy and Titus* (Grand Rapids: Eerdmans, 2018), 309.

7. Ken Sande, *The Peacemaker: A Biblical Guide to Resolving Personal Conflict*, 3rd ed. (Grand Rapids: Baker Books, 2004), 122.

8. Jennie Allen, "BONUS - We Need Each Other," *Made for This with Jennie Allen*, April 23, 2020, podcast transcript, https://www .jennieallen.com/blog/we-need-each-other.

9. Linda Dillow, *Calm My Anxious Heart: A Woman's Guide to Finding Contentment*, 3rd ed. (Colorado Springs: NavPress, 2020), 5.

10. Russell Moore, *The Courage to Stand: Facing Your Fear Without Losing Your Soul* (Nashville: B&H, 2020), 52, 55.

11. Jeffrey A. D. Weima and Steven M. Baugh, *1 & 2 Thessalonians, 1 & 2 Timothy, Titus*, Zondervan Illustrated Bible Backgrounds Commentary (Grand Rapids: Zondervan, 2002), 72.

12. Francis Chan, *Crazy Love: Overwhelmed by a Relentless God* (Colorado Springs: David C Cook, 2013), 64.

13. Michelle Singletary, "How to Gain Financial Freedom," interviewed by Dan Schawbel, *Forbes*, February 2, 2014, https://www .forbes.com/sites/danschawbel/2014/02/02/michelle-singletary -how-to-gain-financial-freedom/?sh=d5aa8d7d4568.

14. Augustine of Hippo, *The Confessions of St. Augustine*, trans. E. B. Pusey (Oak Harbor, WA: Logos Research Systems, 1996), 1.1.1.

15. Weima and Baugh, *1 & 2 Thessalonians, 1 & 2 Timothy, Titus*, 70.

16. Denzel Washington, "Dillard University 2015 Commencement Address," May 9, 2015, Dillard University, New Orleans, LA, YouTube video, 12:10, https://www.youtube.com/watch?v=ROiNPU wg9bQ.

17. Michelle Singletary, *Your Money and Your Man: How You and Prince Charming Can Spend Well and Live Rich* (New York: Ballantine Books, 2006), xiv.

18. Priscilla Shirer, *The Resolution for Women* (Nashville: B&H, 2011), 28.

**Lesson 9**

1. Philip H. Towner, *The Letters to Timothy and Titus*, New International Commentary on the New Testament (Grand Rapids: Eerdmans, 2006), 406.

2. John White, *The Fight* (Downers Grove, IL: InterVarsity, 1977), back cover.

3. Dolly Parton, "The way I see it, if you want the rainbow, you gotta put up with the rain!," Twitter, April 4, 2013, https://twitter.com /dollyparton/status/319869370727796736?lang=en.

4. C. T. Studd, "Only One Life," accessed December 12, 2022, https://tonycooke.org/stories-and-illustrations/only-one-life.

5. Jim Elliot, *The Journals of Jim Elliot*, ed. Elisabeth Elliot (Grand Rapids: Revell, 2002), October 28, 1949.

6. Corrie ten Boom, quoted in Pamela Rosewell Moore, *The Five Silent Years of Corrie ten Boom* (Grand Rapids: Zondervan, 1986), 25–26.

7. Walter C. Smith, "Immortal, Invisible, God Only Wise" (1867), public domain.

8. William D. Mounce, *Pastoral Epistles*, Word Biblical Commentary, vol. 46 (Nashville: Thomas Nelson, 2000), 369.

# Organic
## MENTORING

A MENTOR'S
GUIDE TO
RELATIONSHIPS
WITH NEXT
GENERATION
WOMEN

### SUE EDWARDS & BARBARA NEUMANN

"I love this book! I will definitely incorporate it into several contexts, including my seminary classroom teaching as well as personal relationships. Generational differences have clearly stalled the mentoring advantage. *Organic Mentoring* gets us moving again in a world that desperately needs the benefit of intergenerational mentoring."

—Bev Hislop, Professor of Pastoral Care, Western Seminary, and author of *Shepherding a Woman's Heart* and *Shepherding Women in Pain*

KREGEL
MINISTRY

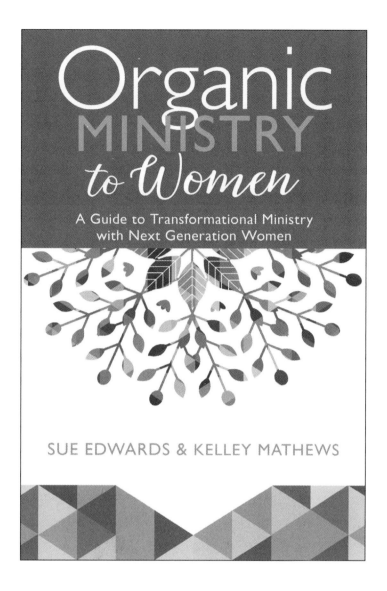

Drawing on decades of experience ministering to women, authors Sue Edwards and Kelley Mathews explain how their Transformation Model can energize women's ministry for all generations and in multiple settings. *Organic Ministry to Women* is packed with practical advice and real-life illustrations of how to implement the principles of the Transformation Model. Edwards and Mathews also profile numerous leading women's ministers like Jen Wilkin, Priscilla Shirer, and Jackie Hill-Perry, drawing wisdom and inspiration from their lives and ministries. Helpful appendixes provide additional resources including sample job descriptions for ministry leaders, a Bible study lesson, and a training guide for small group leaders.

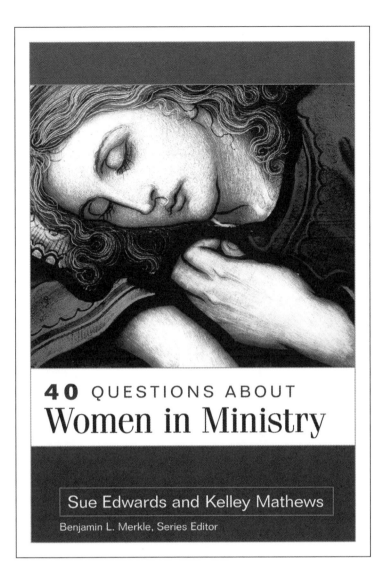

**40** QUESTIONS ABOUT
# Women in Ministry

Sue Edwards and Kelley Mathews

Benjamin L. Merkle, Series Editor

*40 Questions About Women in Ministry* charts a course for understanding differing views on the topic. The accessible question-and-answer format guides readers through specific areas of confusion, and the authors helpfully zero in on the foundations of varied beliefs and practices. Sue Edwards and Kelley Mathews cover interpretive, theological, historical, and practical matters such as What did God mean by the woman as man's "helper"? How is it that Christians reach different conclusions about 1 Tim. 2:11–15? and How did Western culture influence women's roles in society and church?

KREGEL
ACADEMIC